Christianity Made Simple

To Stewart B. Simms, Jr.,
my brother, whose workmanship
in studying and preaching
the Bible has always set a
high standard.

Christianity Made Simple

The Message of Paul's Letter to the

Romans

by Robert Simms

Unless otherwise marked, all scriptures are from the
King James Version of the Bible.

ISBN: 978-0-9834642-7-3
Published in the United States by
Robert F. Simms
Greer, South Carolina

Reading Romans Simply

After attending six months of weekly Bible studies in the New Testament book of 1 Corinthians, a church member rose in a question and answer session to make a comment. "I reckon those Corinthians must have been smarter than us," he said.

"How's that?" asked the pastor.

"Well," the man continued, "I suppose when they got this letter they probably sat down and read it all in one sitting, and understood it. We've been studying it for six months now, and still don't know what it says."[1]

It's possible to make anything more complicated than it is. Bible books in particular seem to suffer wounds from theologically heavy hands. Complex outlines, deeply involved arguments, a maze of citations, and jargon-laden language often obscure the very material the writer is trying to explain. This writer is not innocent of such crimes himself.

Scholars expect complex treatments of simple subjects and make it their business to know how to wade through it all, and enjoy it. Most people, however, have other day jobs and appreciate being able to read something that is challenging without its being tedious.

Romans is one of the richest books in the whole Bible. The range of its topics alone covers the vast spectrum of the Christian faith. And its notable treatments of various of these topics, like the problem of sin, the spiritual nature of human life, the grace of God, election, and God's sovereignty, have been the subjects of untold volumes of exegesis, commentary, and devotional works through the centuries of Christian history.

Why, then, add another book to the shelves? This little book will likely add nothing unique. It isn't intended to be scholarly. Its prose will not be classic or particularly beautiful. In fact, every attempt has been made to keep this book from being too heavy or too flowery.

---

[1] Source unknown

The whole point of this book is to treat Romans in a sweeping fashion, taking in the scope of the letter a chapter at a time, in very little space, and to convince the reader that Paul's letter is not so impenetrable that six months—or even six days—of reading would be necessary to understand it in a basic way. An ancillary purpose of this book is to restate the enduring message of Romans so that it connects to the way modern people organize their thought.

There are countless outlines of Romans. This book will not propose another. Nevertheless, the semblance of an outline will emerge as the inevitable result of dividing the book into chapters and subsections. But the basic outline is that of the chapters of Romans itself, an organization bequeathed to us by those who put the Bible into chapters and verses long after the original authors were dead.

The main purpose of this book, however, is not to convey a new idea about the structure of the book, but to proclaim its message, one more time, in a short space, for regular people.

For years—undoubtedly for centuries—people have intoned the rationalization, 'I don't believe God meant us to understand all of the Bible. I believe there are many parts we won't understand until we get to heaven.' Unquestionably there are parts of the Bible that leave us with a sense of mystery. But if it appears the writer himself understood it, it's meant for the reader to understand as well. Only when the scripture writer clearly sees that what he has said is a mystery, and evokes a doxology of praise to the God who understands all mysteries, should we conclude that we are presumptuous to attempt to comprehend the matter any more fully than he.

To illustrate, frequently the entire book of Revelation is presumed to be beyond our understanding. If so, why was it included in the scripture? Why, indeed, did God inspire its writing? To the contrary, even works as difficult as the apocalypse are meant to be understood, and they actually contain verses promising a special blessing to those who are careful to read and search out their meaning.

The same principle is true of Romans: God intends that we not be intellectually or spiritually lazy, but instead apply our minds and hearts to understanding. This little book on Romans is a humble attempt to promote a simple understanding of a rich and deep book, with the hope that the non-Christian reader may become a Christian, and that the Christian reader may become a more mature and joyful one.

The Deadly Problem of Sin
Romans 1

Religion provides a lot of fodder for jokes, and nothing seems beyond being the butt of humor. One of the older jokes among preachers:

"What are you going to preach on?"

"Sin."

"What are you gonna say about it?"

"I'm agin it!"

Anything can be the topic of jokes. But joking aside, there's nothing funny about sin. People like to make light of sin, because humor reduces tension about the topic. But this is exactly the problem in our society: people don't take seriously the matter of sin.

Many dismiss "sin" as an outdated Bible concept that only outdated religious people believe in. But even among many people who do accept the Bible, the matter of sin is given too little emphasis. Frankly, many Christians are embarrassed to talk about sin as a Bible teaching. In our day, people want to talk about positive things only—Let's make everything light and airy, lovely and wonderful!

But making little of sin makes little of salvation. If sin isn't real, salvation isn't real. If sin isn't serious, salvation isn't significant. If sin isn't damning, salvation isn't necessary. The good news is good because the bad news is really bad: Sin is a deadly condition in which all people are trapped, requiring divine intervention if we are to be saved from its consequences.

Paul begins his letter to the Romans with this message: *The Deadly Problem of Sin.* The heart of the first chapter is verse 18:

18 For the wrath of God is revealed from heaven against all ungodliness and unrighteousness of men, who hold the truth in unrighteousness.

This verse summarizes what the chapter teaches, which is that all people are sinners by nature and by choice, and deserve the wrath of God. God offers salvation to us through the gospel of Jesus Christ, when we are willing to confess our sin and repent from the heart.

Sinners by Nature and by Choice

First, we need to see that we are sinners by nature and by choice.

The Bible begins with the story of Adam and Eve and explains that they chose to do the one thing God told them not to. The result was their fall from their perfect relationship with him, a fall that resulted in spiritual death—on the spot! It infected their souls with a deadly spiritual condition that the Bible then refers to as "sin." And because man when he procreates reproduces body and soul, sin was passed on to all humanity. We were all born with the condition of sin, which gives us a tendency to do wrong from the very start. We also were born without a relationship with God.

Romans doesn't deal with the origins of sin, however; it starts with sin as a fact, speaking of the **"ungodliness and unrighteousness of men"** (v.18), and uses active phrases like **"professing themselves to be wise"** (v.22), **"glorified him not as God"** (v.21), **"changed the glory of the incorruptible God"** (v.23), **"changed the truth of God into a lie"** (v.25), **"change the natural use into that which is against nature"** (v.26), and **"not only do the same, but have pleasure in them that do them"** (v.32). Do you see the sense of these phrases? They describe deliberate choices and intentional actions. They do not describe mistakes. Sin is willful behavior. As a result, Paul says we are **"without excuse"** (v.20). These are not descriptions of just a few people, a horrible minority, exceptions to the rule, as the rest of Romans—and the whole Bible—makes clear. Sin is the condition of all humanity.

We don't like to think of ourselves in these terms. But not liking to doesn't mean we shouldn't confess this truth anyway. We are sinners. We sin. We disobey God. We were born with the tendency, yes, but we have all chosen to disobey God and have done so repeatedly.

Paul begins Romans in this way because the only way for us to understand the importance of the gospel, which the rest of the book explains thoroughly, is to realize the desperate need we are all in. Sin is not a spiritual cold that will go away in 10-14 days. Sin is not a rash that will disappear when external irritants are gone. Sin is not the fault of other people who make us mad. Sin is not a brief lapse of judgment, a passing fancy that we'll grow out of, or even just a set of mistakes which, if we don't repeat them, will be forgotten. Sin is a deadly virus, like HIV, a virus of the soul, whose end is death, and cannot be cured by anything we can do to or for ourselves. New Year's resolutions will not end it. Turning over a new leaf will not cure it. Going to church will not change it. Trying harder will not overcome it. Sin is a deadly condition for which each of us is responsible, and from which we cannot escape on our own. As sinners, we are in desperate need before God.

Deserving the Wrath of God

What makes this condition of sin so serious is that because of our sin, we deserve the wrath of God. People always like to argue that they believe God is loving and would not send people to hell. But that's not what the Bible says. Here in Romans, which agrees with the rest of the Bible, the scripture says, **"The wrath of God is revealed from heaven against all ungodliness and unrighteousness"** (v.18), and further says that people know, in their hearts, that they deserve this wrath: **"Knowing the judgment of God, that they which commit such things are worthy of death"** (v.32).

And make no mistake about it, this "death" is spiritual death, not just physical. Spiritual death is the condition sin has already left us in, which, if it is not resolved, then upon our physical deaths it will result in separation from God forever, in the only place where God does not reside, which is hell.

Until physical death, part of the condemnation of sin is that God will, by his sovereign justice, deal with our sins in sometimes ominous ways. Paul says, **"God also gave them up to uncleanness"** (v.24), **"God gave them up unto vile affections"** (v.26), **"God gave them over to a reprobate mind"** (v.28). Continuation, persistence and willfulness in sinful behavior may result in our being hardened against any change. God may simply withdraw his hand of restraint, and let us go, and it will be nobody's fault but our own.

We know even in the realm of human interaction that we can do only so much to change people's behavior. Some people commit one crime, do time, and never commit crime again. Others are hardened. They hate society and authority even more, and they become worse and worse. When they end up in jail for life, or on an execution gurney, it will be their own fault.

Don't blame God if you exit this life and face condemnation. We deserve death and hell for our sins. It's our own fault.

God Isn't Obliged to Save Us

Furthermore, God isn't obliged to save us from our sins just because we can't save ourselves. We need to see that for all we already know about what God has done, for all the declarations of his love and his best desires for us, God is not under any compulsion to save us. We can't hold him responsible for our condemnation, either because he "let" us sin, or "didn't" save us.

Part of the reason God isn't obliged is that our sin is not an accident. Verse 18 says, **"men...hold the truth in unrighteousness."** This word *hold* in the original language means to suppress. It means that we know what's right but deny it, so we won't be bothered by conscience as we deliberately sin. That's why we are "without excuse." The result is all the horrible sins Paul lists in chapter 1, which include fornication, covetousness, malice, envy, murder, pride, deceit, idolatry and homosexuality. These and other sins are the outworking of the sinful condition of the heart, and for it the Bible says we are **"worthy of death"** (v.32). God doesn't have to save us to be a just God, or even to be a loving God. We can't hold God responsible for our sins, we can't blame him for not saving us, in fact, God's holiness and justice would be satisfied by his letting us die in our sins and perish forever.

We can't stress this enough. Nothing we do, no value we place on ourselves, no argument we make toward God, will force him to save us, or make him the bad guy if we're not finally saved. God is totally righteous and just, and we are not. We are sinners.

This is the deadly problem of sin.

The only solution to it is a gracious act of God. And we find that act in his sending Jesus Christ.

The Gospel is God's Salvation

Paul began his letter to the Romans with greetings and then this statement: "**The gospel of Christ...is the power of God unto salvation to every one that believeth.**" He will shortly explain what "the gospel" means, but even before explaining the matter of sin, Paul has assured us that God, while he isn't obliged to save anyone, has provided a Savior in Jesus Christ. In other words, God gives us the message of hope *even before* he lays before us the deadly problem of sin!

Who Says We're Sinners?

Romans 2

During his ministry on earth, Jesus was brought to anger by few people, but those few included those the Bible says "trusted in themselves that they were righteous, and despised others." Often typified as the scribes and Pharisees, these were people who really thought that their performance as human beings was so much better than all other persons that God would reward them with eternal life. They also go by the biblical name of "hypocrites."

It offended them to be told that they were in as much sin and need as the "sinners" they often referred to critically—the famous "tax collectors and sinners" of the Bible. But if there was to be any hope for them eternally, they had to be confronted with the truth.

And so do we. In the first chapter, we saw that Romans describes the deadly problem of sin. In chapter 2, Paul continues the subject, placing special emphasis on realizing how stealthy sin can be, but how we can recognize it in ourselves, and then how to turn from it.

Notice particularly verse 12, the heart of this chapter, which says:

12 **For as many as have sinned without law shall also perish without law: and as many as have sinned in the law shall be judged by the law.**

Most of us will freely admit we are not perfect. There *are* a few people who defiantly have said, "I've never sinned." Their definitions of sin were strange, but clearly what they meant was that they thought of themselves as being basically without fault. But most of us admit we've done wrong things.

What many people balk at is the term "sin," or "sinner." It sounds so *bad!* Well, it is bad, no question about it. But it isn't restricted to one type of person or another, to the exclusion of any. As Romans 3 will say bluntly, "All have sinned, and come short of the glory of God."

People may say, "Who says I'm a sinner?" On what authority do

Christians present the gospel of Christ which includes, to start off with, the claim that all of us are sinners?

The Whole Bible

To begin with, it is the testimony of the whole Bible.

Paul writes in verses 1-3 that we who judge others—that is, who compare ourselves to others and find *them* to be sinners but not ourselves—that we **"do the same things"** (v.1). And he says that **"We are sure that the judgment of God is according to truth against them which commit such things"** (v.2), referring to his list in the last four verses of chapter 1. That list covered lots of terrible and perverse things, but also disobedience to parents, covetousness, envy, deceit, gossip, and boasting. Does anyone still think any of he's guiltless? To cover all the bases, Paul starts the list with the words, **"*all* unrighteousness."** All.

Paul was just going over well proven points made by the witness of the entire Bible. Whether Genesis with its declaration that"every imagination of the thoughts of his heart was only evil all the time," or Psalms with its statement that God looked for someone good, and could not find anyone, or Isaiah with his description of us all like sheep, going astray, the whole Bible tells us we are all sinners.

It doesn't tell us we're all the same kind of sinners, or that all our sin is threatening to the nation or will bring disaster in physical terms. It simply says we are all sinners, which is why we sin. Sin starts on the inside and works its way out.

James describes it this way: "Every man is tempted when he is drawn away of his own lust, and enticed. Then when lust hath conceived, it bringeth forth sin: and sin, when it is finished, bringeth forth death." The point Paul is making in Romans 2 is that in spite of the fact that some Jews believed they were better than others, the same spirit or infection of sin inhabited their hearts, and they were guilty of their own kind of sins, putting us all on level ground. We're all under condemnation.

And Paul says this indictment of sin is true of people even

apart from knowledge of the Bible. He writes, **"As many as have sinned without [outside] law shall also perish without law."** That meant those "outside" the covenant people, who did not have the Bible as their guide, still had the testimony of conscience, the evidence of God in the world, and other things that sufficiently informed them of right and wrong. And they will be judged on this basis: that even without the Bible, they know what some wrong things are, and they do wrong by choice. All are sinners, period.

The Law of God

Furthermore, and very specifically, the law God gave shows us we are sinners. Paul spends verses 12-27 dealing with the way the law states God's principles of holy living, in such a way that although a person may say, "I don't do such and such," he will have to confess, "but I do commit thus and so."

For instance, verse 21 suggests the idea that some steal from banks or houses, while others steal from God by withholding tithes. Verse 22 implies the fact that some commit adultery with their bodies, risking discovery, while others commit it with their hearts, but still poison their lives.

The fact is, the law is a yardstick that none of us measures up to. We all come short of measuring up to the standard of God.

A son was talking with his father during a weekend home from his sophomore year at college. He was having difficulty being patient with a particular professor's method, which was to assign points to various answers, add them all up, and whoever got the most points got an A, while the one with the least points got an F. The dad told him that's just another way of grading on the curve, the infamous method of assuming that in any class there will be some whose performance is essentially perfect and some who flop and fail. Grades are plotted on a predetermined curve, and most people make C's while one or two at most make an A and the same number fail. It's a potentially miserable system of injustice, because what it really does is pit each student against the other, not against a standard of excellence. It's possible, grading on a curve, that someone who gets 85% to 90% of questions right, will still fail, because everybody else did better. But it also means that if you only get 65% right, but do better than anyone else, you'll get the A.

Interestingly, human beings would like to be graded on a curve eternally—or you'd think so. Because we tend to compare our performance with other people, find ourselves "better then them," and conclude that we'll "pass" and get into heaven. We figure the best we can do is the best that can be done, and the worst anyone of us does is basically the only level deserving condemnation.

But God doesn't grade on a curve. He judges by an absolute standard: his holiness. And his holiness has been represented to us in the law of God. And by that law none of us measures up: we're all sinners.

Your Own Heart

In the final analysis, your own heart bears out what the word of God in general and the law of God specifically says: that you are a sinner.

Paul invites his readers to look honestly at themselves. He asks repeated questions: **Dost thou steal? Dost thou commit adultery? Dost thou commit sacrilege? Dishonorest thou God?** (vv.21-23). Each of us knows he has done wrong. Let's use the Bible word: we have sinned. Probably the three most difficult words to say—I have sinned.

And one other question Paul poses to help us arrive at the right conclusion: **"Despisest thou the riches of his goodness and forbearance and longsuffering; not knowing that the goodness of God leadeth thee to repentance?"** (v.4). In spite of the fact that we are sinners, God has continued to be good to us, meeting needs, helping us through, getting us over, providing. Why? Because it's one of his methods of getting us to recognize he is a loving God, and encouraging us to be honest, confess our sins, and come to him for what he alone can do: forgive us.

This repentance is the only answer. God has provided for Jesus

Christ to pay for our sins on the cross. But the only way we can have the gift of his forgiveness is if we will leave sin behind and come to Christ.

In verses 6-16, Paul appears to be saying some people are good and some are not, but in reality he is describing the differences between those who repent of sin and follow God in Jesus Christ, and those who don't. Those who repent **"seek for glory and honor and immortality, eternal life"** (v.7). They **"work good."** They turn *from* sin, and *to* God, receiving Christ as Lord. In his lordship they do good, live holy, grow spiritually, follow the will of God. They don't receive the reward of heaven because they live in a holy way, they live in a holy way because they have already received the reward of heaven and their lives are changed.

A political candidate some years ago had the slogan, "In your heart, you know he's right." Sometimes after all the evidence is shown, the proof is laid on the table, and the authoritative sources have spoken, it's looking into your own heart that convinces you. Because even if the arguments are flawless, and we have no place else to go logically, if we deny the truth in our hearts, we will not be convinced by arguments of the mind. And it's in the heart that God works and to the heart that God speaks. It's there he does his work to convince you and me that we are sinners needing his grace.

That's why it's not wise for any Christian—preacher or "layman"—to manipulate people into making decisions. If God is not speaking to their hearts, no one should attempt to squeeze out a decision by manipulating their emotions.

God does speak to our hearts, however, and there are many persons who have heard the gospel, and who have sensed deep within themselves that it is the voice of the Lord. Some of these folks attend church occasionally, out of a vague and nagging sense of need. Some avoid church like the plague, though they cannot escape the ever present feeling of needing something more than they have, something real and eternal. They know they have sinned, and need forgiveness. And until we confess our need of Christ, the gospel, in all its power to save, will not save us.

There is a danger that if we resist too long, what Paul describes in v.5 will come true:

> **5   But after thy hardness and impenitent heart treasurest up unto thyself wrath against the day of wrath and revelation of the righteous judgment of God.**

But Paul's goal is not to threaten, but to invite. As a preacher of the wonderful gospel of Christ, he invites us to listen to our hearts, where God speaks, to consider the law, and the whole word of God, and to confess our own condition, that we're sinners, in need of a Savior.

But For The Grace Of God

Romans 3

There's an old saying, expressive of humility, that when you see someone in the gutter, you should say, "There but for the grace of God go I." This is a confession that ultimately God is in sovereign control over the lot of humanity and every individual. And it's a very biblical principle.

From our perspective, we human beings have free will. We know we make choices, we know what happens to us is related to those choices, and we rightly conclude that our free will is not an illusion. We are not puppets who only appear to be free. The Bible tells us, "Choose you this day whom you will serve," and we believe God means this is a real choice.

From God's eternal perspective, however, the whole of creation's history is already fact, and every life and every choice in every life is both known to him, and in some mysterious way that only he understands, is part of his sovereign plan.

In consequence, anything good we experience is due to the grace of God—even those things we think we did for ourselves.

"I made my own fortune," a person may say, but it is God's grace that he did. If God had not enabled him, perhaps in hundreds of ways, it would not have happened.

"I keep myself healthy," a person may say, but if not for the grace of God, unavoidable, incurable illness may have struck.

But most important of all, if human beings are to live eternally with God in heaven, it will only be by the grace of God. This is the repeated message of the Bible.

The third chapter of Romans is about this grace of God without which we have no eternal hope. The core verses of this chapter are 23-24, which say:

23 **For all have sinned, and come short of the glory of God;**
24 **Being justified freely by his grace through the redemption that is in Christ Jesus.**

These two short verses summarize the eternally lost condition of all human beings before God, and the single thing that can change that condition to one of eternal life and glory—the grace of God. There are three major emphases in this chapter that teach us what this grace means.

I Would Be Condemned Still

The first is that *but for the grace of God,* I would be condemned still—condemned in sin and because of sin.

We Are All Sinners

First of all, we're all sinners. Chapters 1-2 took up this subject at great length, and Paul repeats the conclusion in verse 23: **"All have sinned."** He also quotes extensively from the Psalms, where David tells the brutal truth about the rebellious heart of man.

We Are To Blame

Second, we are to blame for our sin, not God. Verses 1-8 tell us that even the Jews, to whom God revealed himself specially, sinned greatly. And even though God uses a person's—or a whole nation's—waywardness to glorify him somehow, we cannot blame him for our disobedience. That God sovereignly plans history and uses all of it to glorify himself is his business, and he is totally righteous in it. But we are still accountable for our choices. **"Let God be true, but every man a liar,"** Paul says, perhaps thinking of Job 40:8, where God says to Job, "Wilt thou condemn me, that thou mayest be righteous?"

We Are All Under Judgment

Since we are sinners, we are under the judgment of God. Verse 9 poses the question of whether anyone is *not* under the judgment of God. **"Are *we* [Jews] any better than *they* [Gentiles]? No, in no wise, for we have before proved both Jews and Gentiles, that they are all under sin."**

We know we are under judgment because of sin because, as

verse 20 says, **"by the law is the knowledge of sin."** When we look at God's law, we know we have not kept it perfectly.

Sin must be paid for. Romans 1:23 said bluntly that all we sinners are **"worthy of death."** And here in 3:20 Paul writes, **"By the deeds of the law there shall no flesh be justified in his sight."** We cannot be righteous in God's sight even by being as good as we can be. It's not enough.

We're in a predicament, aren't we? We're all "in sin"—sinners. The penalty for sin is death. If not interrupted, it will overtake us with eternal finality.

Recently a program appeared on television showing dramatic rescues. One episode was about a challenging, dangerous white-water run, which most kayakers and canoers will navigate only by getting out of their craft and walking it through. One brave, or foolhardy soul, though, giddily wearing a Viking helmet for effect, ploughed into the rapids to show it could be done. Halfway through, his boat wedged between rocks and turned on its side, facing upstream. He was stuck inside it, bobbing up to the surface for air, calling for help. The water rushing from behind, however, hit him in such a way that it forced him under, and soon he disappeared from view, still stuck in the submerged hull.

Were it not for someone nearby who braved death himself to pull the would-be Viking out, he would have died, and indeed, when pulled free, he was not breathing. He was seconds from death.

That's our condition in sin. We are headed down life's river, already dangerous because of its steady rush to its conclusion. Sin has already brought us under its condemnation, and we will all go through the rapids of physical death. But if we go through as sinners, commanding our own craft, lord of our own lives, thinking we can survive by ourselves, sin will bury us in eternal judgment.

We need someone to pull us free. And but for the grace of God, I would be condemned still. But because of the grace of God,

I Have A Savior In Jesus

He's the life saver standing by, watching me descend that stream of death. And God sent him to save me, and you.

The Bible says we are **"justified freely by his grace through the redemption that is in Christ Jesus: Whom God hath set forth to be a propitiation through faith in his blood, to declare his righteousness for the remission of sins that are past, through the forbearance of God."**

Let's take that one phrase at a time:

Justified freely by his grace means that God decides to save us for no other reason than that's the kind of God he is, and he offers this rescue from judgment on our sins as a *gift,* free for the receiving of it.

Through the redemption that is in Christ Jesus means that God accomplished this rescue through Jesus Christ. There is no other savior, none. "There is no other name under heaven, given among men, whereby we must be saved" (Acts 4:12).

Whom God hath set forth to be a propitiation through faith in his blood means that Jesus' blood, his death on the cross, was the payment for the sins of us all. In his six hours of separation from the Father on the cross, the eternal Son suffered the equal of what you and each of us would suffer in hell for eternity. We cannot imagine how profound his suffering was. And it was a propitiation, a payment, for our sins.

Through faith means that the way we receive the benefits of his death for us is simply to trust him to save us, to give up all other hopes, all other methods, all other beliefs, all other worship, and to trust him alone to be our Savior. To throw our whole weight upon him, welcoming him into our lives as Lord.

To declare his righteousness for the remission of sins means that God's righteousness is satisfied in the blood of Christ, and because of it, our sins can be remitted—we can be forgiven.

The illustration of lifesaving is helpful to us further. Lifeguards are taught that in saving people who are drowning, they must grasp them in a way that the victim can't drown them both.

Drowning people frequently fight lifeguards. They do so because they don't trust their saviors, but in their frenzy and fear they are trying to climb on top of them for buoyancy. In essence, they are still trying to save themselves, and are not letting the lifeguard save them.

Here's what God says we must do with Jesus: trust him. Trust him implicitly. Trust him completely. Trust him only. Let go, and let God. Let Christ save you.

This is what the balance of Romans 3 is about:

I Receive God's Grace By Faith

Grace is God's offer. Faith is our acceptance. Grace is his salvation. Faith is the means by which we receive it. Grace is his goodness toward us. Faith is our response.

Verse 26 says God justifies **"him which believeth in Jesus."** We have to realize that "believe" and "faith" are the same word in the Greek of the New Testament. One is a verb, the other a noun. We don't have an English word "to faith," but we should.

Verse 28 says, **"a man is justified by faith without the deeds of the law."** That is, God makes you right with him when you trust in Christ, not because you have lived a good life—because in fact, none of us is good enough to be saved.

Faith is one of the simplest things in the world. Even animals can express a certain kind of faith. A confirmed cat owner said, "My cat is never afraid we'll step on him or kick him aside, because we never have, and even when we nearly run into each other in a hall or doorway, we step to the side of each other—I always have. And since in the human world, traffic keeps to the right (in America) I always step to my right, and he does, too, just like he had good sense. And we never pulled his tail, so he doesn't mind our stroking it. We never mistreated him, so he isn't afraid or skittish like some cats are."

That cat's behavior is really just an animal version of faith. He trusts us because we are trustworthy.

Little babies come into the world crying, but as soon as they have had enough interaction with other people, if they have decent parents, they learn to trust them. In fact, they trust them so completely that parents can't help but become profoundly aware of how important it is that they keep their word and provide well. Having children makes most people more responsible, because they see the faith children place in them.

God wants us to trust him, because he is trustworthy. He has never mistreated us. We have disrespected and mistreated ourselves, we have perverted God's purposes, we have sinned and brought death into the world he created perfect and good. We have been violent, unjust, mean, deceitful, selfish, bitter, angry, rebellious, wandering. But God is always good. And in Jesus he has sent us his very best, a Savior to keep us from being eternally condemned. He has done all the work for us. All he asks us to do to be saved is to turn from sin and every other idea of salvation, then open our hearts, and receive his gift.

Why, God even provides the desire to turn around, and the ability to believe him. If you feel you should turn to Christ, if you feel like placing your trust in him, it's God at work, by his grace, leading you to himself. Philippians 2:13 says, "It is God which worketh in you both to will and to do of his good pleasure." God supplies the what to, the how to, and the want to.

We can't get away from it: But for the grace of God, we were all hopelessly condemned. But for the grace of God, there would be no remedy for sin and death and hell. But because of the grace of God, there is. His name is Jesus. Do you know him? Is he yours, and are you his?

How Can You Be Saved?

Romans 4

Once people realize that their lives are brief, and come to recognize that human beings do not disappear into non-existence but go on in another state after death, then people want to know, where will I go? How and where will I spend eternity?

The plain message of the Bible is that after death we will reside in either heaven or hell, and that which one it is depends on whether or not we have been "saved." Saved from what?

The answer of Paul in Romans is twofold: from the condition, and the condemnation, of sin.

The natural condition of man in this world, ever since Adam and Eve, is sin—rebellion against God. If this condition does not change, it results in final condemnation and separation from God, which is hell. And the only change that can take place in this condition is by what the Bible calls salvation, or being saved. Salvation is a work of God, by which he brings a person to an awareness of personal sin, repentance and confession of sin, then a recognition of Jesus Christ as the Son of God and the only Savior, and surrender to and receipt of Jesus Christ as Lord. In the resulting relationship with Christ: a person is forgiven of sin; he is given a new, spiritual birth so that he can know God and serve him; and he receives the Holy Spirit of God, to secure his eternal life and make Christ real to him.

Personal salvation is absolutely necessary if one is to spend eternity in heaven. So how can you be saved?

The heart of Romans 4 is verse 16, which neatly sums up the pathway to salvation, the details of which are explained by the rest of this and succeeding chapters:

16 **Therefore** *it is* **of faith, that it might be by grace; to the end the promise might be sure to all the seed; not to that only which is of the law, but to that also which is of the faith of Abraham; who is the father of us all...**

In the first chapters of Romans, Paul laid out bluntly and powerfully the case for the deadly problem of sin, and he told us just who it is who says we're sinners—God and his word. But then Paul wrote that because of the grace of God, we who would otherwise be lost and without hope, have a Savior offered to us.

In Romans 4, Paul now lays out clearly how one is saved. He makes three points, two to clear up misunderstandings, and one to explain simply how to be saved.

Salvation has always been a gift received through faith

The first thing to clear up is any misunderstanding about the nature of salvation. Most people have some idea that if they're "good," they'll go to heaven, and if they're "bad," they won't. This idea is the invention of the sinful human mind, but it attempts to quote the Bible to support it. In fact, Romans 2 said, "[God] will render to every man according to his deeds…" The passage goes on to mention those who do well and those who do not obey the truth. But such passages are pulled out of their contexts and distorted. In fact, Revelation 20:12-13 shows that those who finally are going to be judged by their works are only "the dead," meaning those who die unsaved. And there is only one judgment that can be rendered in that case: eternal punishment.

Paul lays out clearly here in Romans that salvation has always been a gift received by faith, and never a reward for good works.

The Jews had come to believe otherwise, of course, but Paul proves them wrong, using the example of the one whom all Israel revered: Abraham. In vv.1-8 he says that Abraham did not glory before God for anything he had done, but that he **"believed God, and it was counted unto him for righteousness."** Paul says if someone is rewarded for his works, the matter of grace is not involved. Since we have repeated definitions of salvation as being "by grace," we have to conclude that works have nothing to do with it. A thing is either deserved or not, earned or not. Salvation isn't earned. It's a gift. And gifts must be received by faith.

Paul looked back in the Bible and saw the word **"counted"** with reference to Abraham, and he noted David's saying something about "**imputed**." He seized on these words, telling us that the Bible teaches from the earliest that salvation is when God does not *impute* our sins to us (meaning, he doesn't count them against us), but rather that he *counts* or considers us righteous on the basis of his grace and our acceptance of it by faith.

Paul summarized the point about the futility of trying to earn salvation in Romans 4:15: **"Because the law worketh wrath."** This is the function of the law: it condemns sin. If we had never broken the law, and if we could continue to flawlessly obey God's law—all of it—through our dying breaths, the result might be different. But we have all sinned, broken the law, and rebelled against God. The only thing the law does now is show us we have sinned and judge us to be condemned and needing salvation if we are to have any hope. And this salvation has always been on the basis of grace through faith.

Some say the Old Testament shows salvation by works, and the New Testament shows salvation by faith. This is untrue. Some say the Old Testament God is angry and demanding, and the New Testament God is gracious and forgiving. This is also untrue. God has always been what he is now and ever shall be, and the Old Testament shows he is a loving God who simply does not put up with sin. In both Testaments God has the same standard of holiness, judges sin the same way, holds sinners accountable in the same way, and offers salvation in the same way: believe him and surrender to him, and your faith will enable you to receive the gift of salvation.

You don't join the church to be saved; you join the church because you are saved

The second misunderstanding to clear up is about the connection of joining a church to the matter of salvation. The simple fact is, you can't join a church and become saved as a result. That's backwards. You don't join the church to be saved; you join the church because you *are* saved. There are clubs for twins. If you joined one of them, it would not make you a twin, if you weren't already one.

God wants his saved people to be part of his church, yes, but we have to get the order straight. First we deal with God about sin and salvation. We must be born spiritually to eternal life. Then once that's settled, we can join a church of the Lord Jesus Christ.

In vv.9-14 Paul is answering the question as to whether being a Jew, being circumcised, being an official part of the community of Jewish faith, is required before you can be saved. He disproves this idea, showing that Abraham, the father of the Jewish faith, was declared by God to be "righteous" (meaning, right with God or saved), *before* he was circumcised, and that he was circumcised only afterward, as a sign of his relationship to God. In other words, his salvation came first, and his joining the "church" of his day (he was its first member!) came second, as a result.

People try to make baptism this same thing, a ritual that saves them. But baptism is like circumcision in that it is only an outward sign of an inward reality. If you haven't been saved, joining the church and being baptized won't do the trick.

Dwight Moody once said, "Whitewashing the pump won't make the water pure." What a dangerous thing it is to hold out hope that being baptized, or having been a member of a church, will mean anything to God when you die and stand before him, if there has been no spiritual experience of salvation, no entry of the Spirit of God, no deliverance from sin, no relationship to Christ.

Salvation is by God's grace through our faith

If we can't get to heaven by what we've done, or for what we haven't done, and if joining the church doesn't save us, what does? Salvation is by God's grace, through our faith. That's the only way.

There are two parts to this. Let's look at them simply:

1. God's grace is his gift of forgiveness and eternal life through what Jesus has already done.

Paul explains in vv.24-25 that God "**raised up Jesus our Lord from the dead; who was delivered for our offences, and was raised again for our justification.**" Without explaining these events in detail, Paul simply alludes to the gospel as it was preached and written about. Jesus died on the cross for our sins. He came to this world for this purpose, to die for us, to be our substitute. When he died, he paid the penalty for our sins, all of them, forever. And he broke sin's power so that we could live for God.

2. Faith means taking God at his word, receiving Christ as Savior, surrendering to him as Lord. To place faith in Jesus means first

- You believe he is who he said he was and who the Bible testifies he was: God the Word made flesh, God the Son.
- You believe that Jesus died for your sins and that he was raised from the dead. The New Testament proves this and repeats it urgently for us to believe.
- You receive Jesus by invitation to your life to be your Savior. Just like inviting a guest at your door to come in, you can receive Jesus in prayer.
- You accept and surrender to the Lordship of Jesus over your life. Just as submitting to military service commits you to obey officers, so receiving Jesus commits you to consider him your head and authority.

Paul tells us something very important in Romans 4:16, that God makes salvation by grace instead of by law so that it can be for everyone, not only Jews, but also Gentiles. In other words, he makes salvation an act of his goodness received as a gift through our simple trust, so that anyone can be saved: not only people who grew up religious, but also those who didn't; not only those who grew up in the Christian faith to begin with, but also those who grew up hating it or just not knowing anything about it; not only those who have lived lives that are relatively moral and ethical, but also those who grew up on the wrong side of what's right and good altogether.

For the truth is that one born into religion, morality, and general knowledge of the Bible needs Jesus Christ as much as the one who didn't. And God has made it possible for anyone to be saved, just by receiving the gift. It doesn't matter where you've wandered, what you've done, what you believed. If you will leave it all behind, give your life to Jesus Christ, and receive his salvation by faith, you *will* be saved.

How can we say this? On the authority of the word of God, the Bible. It says that salvation will be given as a gift to us, **"if we believe on him that raised up Jesus our Lord from the dead; who was delivered for our offences, and was raised again for our justification (vv.24-25)."**

The foregoing simple explanation of how to be saved is really all a person needs to know to escape the condemnation of sin, be transferred from the power of darkness to the kingdom of the Son of God (Col. 1:13) and have assurance of eternal life. But most of us want to have more than the simplest knowledge and understanding of things. We want to know how they work. It's no different with salvation, especially since a Christian will face criticism, skepticism, religious ideas that conflict with the gospel, people who deny the truth of the Bible and even people who will deliberately and maliciously try to destroy a new Christian's faith by attacking it at any vulnerable point. Nothing exposes vulnerability more than ignorance, so knowing more of the Bible's teaching about grace and faith is important.

In Romans 5, Paul turns to a little deeper explanation of the concept of grace.

Just How Grace Works

Romans 5

Are you a "fix-it" person? Fix-it people like to know how things work—even if they're not broken.

When it comes to spiritual things, too, people are frequently curious about how they "work." Some things must be accepted on the basis of faith without fully understanding them. Don't demand a course on electricity before simply flipping a light switch. But then it's valuable to study things to see just how they work. God is a God of order and design, after all.

Sometimes when people are faced with the gospel, they wonder how God can forgive sins "just like that." We know that we don't forgive that easily, and we tend to project upon God our own prejudices and sinful attitudes. The Bible says God is full of love and grace, and that he offers salvation as a gift to us, free for the receiving. In one sense, it is very costly—we must give him our lives in surrender to Jesus as Lord. But we don't have to pay anything, do anything to earn it, spend any time doing penance, or anything like that. When the gospel is told to us, we can decide from the heart to truly repent of our sin, receive God's offer, or not, and if we receive it, we will be forgiven of sin and saved eternally, "just like that." How can that be? How does that work?

Romans 5 tells us just how grace works. The heart of that chapter is in vv.8-9:

8 But God commendeth his love toward us, in that, while we were yet sinners, Christ died for us.
9 Much more then, being now justified by his blood, we shall be saved from wrath through him.

How are we saved? In chapter 4 of Romans, Paul essentially said, look folks, it's either by works or by grace. We can't be saved by our works, because our sins have put us behind, and we can't catch up no matter how much we do. It has to be by grace, and only grace, no mixture of grace and works—God's goodness and our good living. It has to be all God's doing, or we won't be saved at all.

Now in chapter 5 he explains how grace "works."

Grace is God's Sovereign Plan

First, grace is God's sovereign plan—how he chose from before the foundation of the world to accomplish our salvation. And in this plan, we see three things:

1. The Price is Paid in Love

First, the price is paid in love. God sent Christ to take the penalty of sin for us. Verse 6 says, **"For when we were without strength, in due time Christ died for the ungodly...God commendeth his love toward us in that while we were yet sinners, Christ died for us."** This can only be God's love, because "sinners" means we were not deserving of it, and in fact it implies all that took place when Jesus was crucified—the rejection, the forsaking, the judgment, the false condemnation of Jesus, the spitting, the nailing, the cursing. Some people hid in the shadows. The worst people shouted and whipped and nailed Jesus to a cross. But all humanity past and future helped put him there, because all people had sinned and as long as there is a human race all people will sin. God, however, loved you and me enough to become one of us and die for our sins.

Rembrandt's moving painting, "The Raising of the Cross," depicts the figure of Christ on the cross, various persons raising the cross upright, and a person of authority overseeing. In the shadows, however, Rembrandt painted himself as one of the people watching nearby. The painter knew that even though he lived sixteen hundred years later than Jesus, he was just as responsible for the crucifixion as anyone before him, or anyone after. It was sin that placed Jesus on the cross, and all who sin are part of his team of executioners.

2. The Victory is Complete

Not only was the salvation that God accomplished in Jesus paid for in love, but also our victory through him is complete.

The chapter opens with three phenomenal blessings that are ours in Christ when we're saved:

- We have peace with God (v.1). This is an enormous gift. We are right with God, at peace with God; God smiles on us; we are in his favor.
- We have access to God (v.2). Through faith, we can approach God, speak with him, hear from him, receive from his hand of grace, because we have this standing with him *by* his grace.
- We have joy in Christ (v.2). Knowing we are forgiven and are going to heaven is continual reason to rejoice. Salvation puts all the troubles of this earth in perspective.

3. Our Troubles are Redeemed

For the saved person, not only are the good things great, but even the "bad" things that happen in our lives are redeemed by God. That is, he takes and uses the trouble and tribulation for good purposes, to make better Christians of us, and to glorify his name.

Verses 3-5 tell us that tribulations make us patient, that patience gives us experience, and that out of our growing experience with God comes an assurance of his blessing, now and eternally. This also is God's grace: he is good to us even in the midst of what seem like bad things.

So God's plan is to show us his grace, his unmerited goodness, first in saving us, then in crowning our lives with great victory, and in saving us daily through troubles, until we finally see him and all sins and troubles will be everlastingly gone.

One of the pretty songs from "The Sound of Music" is called, "I Must Have Done Something Good." Captain Von Trapp and Maria fall in love and at one point they sing to each other this song, saying back and forth to one another, "Nothing comes from nothing, nothing ever could, so somewhere in my youth, or childhood, I must have done something good." The philosophy is clear: anything good that happens to me must be a reward for something I have done to deserve it, even if long ago.

Perhaps such a philosophy seems valid occasionally; however, it isn't so with salvation. Because even if God rewarded our good living, the judgment on our sin would outweigh it. We would always come out losing. It has to be by grace that God saves us, or we wouldn't be saved. Thank God that his sovereign plan has always been to save us by his grace.

So grace works first by being God's sovereign plan—that's simply the way he wanted to do it. What brought about this plan?

Sin Necessitated God's Grace

Put simply, sin made God's grace necessary if we were to be saved at all. If we were left in sin, left to what would happen to us because of our sin, if we were finally judged by the balance of our goodness vs. our sin, then none of us would be saved. If God were to have us for himself, to fulfill his creative purpose in putting us here, he would have to save us by grace.

Verses 12-21 are a back-and-forth comparison of the case of sin vs. grace, or death vs. life, or Adam vs. Christ. Basically Paul takes the comparison and turns it around like a cube and describes it from every possible perspective. He summarizes the same thoughts in 1 Corinthians 15:21-22:

> **For since by man came death, by man came also the resurrection of the dead. For as in Adam all die, even so in Christ shall all be made alive.**

Here in Romans 5, he basically says that sin creates a trap that ends in death, from which there is no escape without the salvation of Christ. Let's string together only the parts of verses 11-21 that deal with the sin problem:

> **12 By one man sin entered into the world, and death by sin; and so death passed upon all men, for that all have**

sinned. 15 ...Through the offense of one many are dead. 18...By the offense of one, judgment came upon all men to condemnation. 19...By one man's disobedience many were made sinners. 20...Sin abounded. 21...Sin hath reigned unto death.

Paints a rather bleak picture, doesn't it? This is the problem that made grace necessary. God would have to pardon us on the basis of something he alone could do, For we can do nothing alone but sin and die.

Just before President Clinton left office in 2001, he issued quite a few pardons. Every president can pardon people, and perhaps all of them do. President Ford created controversy when he issued a pardon to outgoing President Nixon, so as to keep the Watergate affair from poisoning his own presidency and the future.

People debated some of Clinton's pardons on merits, but the principle of the pardon itself is sound, and has been upheld by almost all civilized governments for millennia: those with sufficient power can demonstrate the wonderful quality of grace and release persons from any responsibility for crimes they may have committed. A pardon wipes the slate clean. They are free.

We find it difficult to believe, too, and perhaps we wonder how God can do it, but God has the power and authority, and he chooses to pardon us. He forgives us, and saves us from the penalty of our sins, simply by his grace.

But *how* does he do it? That's what we've been trying to answer. We've seen that his grace works by sovereign plan, and because there is no other way for us to be saved. But exactly how?

Christ Died for our Sins

Let's look at the same verses we just looked at where Adam and Christ were compared, and let's take just the parts where Christ's salvation is described:

11...Through our Lord Jesus Christ we have now received

the atonement. 15...The grace of God, and the gift by grace, which is by one man, Jesus Christ, hath abounded unto many. 16...The free gift is of many offenses unto justification. 17...They which receive abundance of grace and of the gift of righteousness shall reign in life by one, Jesus Christ. 19...By the obedience of one shall many be made righteous. 20...Where sin abounded, grace did much more abound. 21...Grace reigns through righteousness unto eternal life by Jesus Christ our Lord.

One man, Adam, got us all in trouble through sin. But God's man Jesus Christ, the God-Man, saves us by his perfect life and sacrificial death, and by his resurrection from the dead. Seen as one great act or work of salvation, what Christ did brought us the gift of forgiveness and eternal life.

Paul is careful to say repeatedly that where one sin brought death to *all*, Christ's work brought salvation to *many*. He does this for a very important reason. Not all people everywhere are saved by Jesus' work. Only those who receive the gift (vv.15,16,17,18) are saved through Christ's death and resurrection. So, the chapter ends on this note: **"That as sin hath reigned unto death, even so *might* grace reign through righteousness unto eternal life by Jesus Christ our Lord.** In other words, you can and *will* be saved, and you can and *will* have eternal life, only *if* Jesus Christ is your Lord. It's all conditioned on your acceptance of God's gift by repentance and faith.

So grace works because that's simply how God decided to do it, and because there was no other way. Grace works specifically by God's providing Christ to die in our place, so we could receive the gift of salvation.

Every normal American has had thoughts of "what if" he won the Publisher's Clearing House Sweepstakes. Practically every American receives one or more letters from Publishers Clearing House in December and January urging him to enter the sweepstakes, and of course, to buy magazines. Millions of people watch the Super Bowl the last Sunday in January, during which the winner of the sweepstakes typically has been announced. How many of us, do you suppose, if we had answered the doorbell to the sight of a big, multi-million dollar check, would have said, "No thanks, I didn't do anything to deserve it, so I'll have to pass, at least until I think I've done something worthy." Sounds stupid, doesn't it?

However, people do the equivalent thing all the time with the gospel, the good news that Jesus Christ has died for sins and risen to life, and that simply by opening our hearts in repentance and taking by faith the gift of eternal life, we will be saved. Some people think, "I'm not ready. I'm not worthy. I need to clean up a bit, I have to stop this or start that first." Is that any less foolish than refusing $10 million?

Some people aren't really thinking rationally; instead, they're yielding to Satan's temptation. He plants the strong suggestion in a person's mind and heart that he doesn't need to repent or that he simply isn't ready.

Some people know they are just making excuses, but they really believe they need to "help God out" by at least earning *some* of the gift of salvation.

But that's not how grace works. Grace works by being totally the plan of God to give us something we don't deserve and never could, something only Jesus Christ could accomplish for us, and did accomplish, something offered to us simply for the receiving.

Can you think of any good reason that you wouldn't accept that kind of offer?

Our concern with earning salvation by good living—good works—may be an honest misconception of what salvation requires or simply a mask for pride and rebellion. However, Paul did not intend for his readers to get the idea that righteous living was not a concern of God's at all. It was a matter of the cart and the horse. In this case, good works have nothing to do with salvation, but everything to do with Christian living—what comes after salvation is received.

Once you have accepted God's offer of salvation by grace
through faith, *then* you can turn some attention to worthy living,
in response to the goodness of God in saving you. Paul wrote in
Ephesians 2:10, "We are his workmanship, created in Christ Jesus
unto good works..." We are not saved *by* good living, but we are
saved so that we *can* live worthily unto God and bring him praise.
In Romans 6, Paul now turns to how saved people can live above
sin.

Living Above Sin
Romans 6

A pastor preached a sermon based on Galatians 5:16 entitled, "The Secret to Perfection." That verse says: "Walk in the Spirit and ye shall not fulfil the lust of the flesh." A deacon came up to the pastor afterwards and told him bluntly that he strongly opposed what he said, because he didn't believe anyone could be perfect. The pastor patiently told him that's not what he was saying in the sermon, and that in fact he had stated that very clearly.

What the pastor *did* say was that the Bible gives us the secret to living above sin, of having victory over sin, through the full dimension of God's leading and power. Essentially, as long as Christ is having full victory over you and in you, you will experience full victory over temptation, and you will not sin. This is the blunt message of Galatians 5:16. Unless that deacon wanted to contest the plain sense of the scripture, he had no ground to stand upon.

This story illustrates that many people, including Christians, who should know better, have resigned themselves to their sins, thinking there is no real victory in Christian living, no real hope of holiness in their lives.

Whether their resignation to sinfulness is because people secretly don't want to forsake sins, don't want to expend the spiritual energy to get victory, or really and truly because they are not aware that such victory can be had, who can say.

What we can say is that the Bible teaches us how to overcome temptation and avoid or refuse to sin. We can reasonably predict that even knowing how to do this, and practicing it more and more, we will still sin as long as we are in this flesh. Nevertheless, we should learn how God has planned for us to overcome sin. Because God wants us to sin less, be holy more, and grow into the likeness of Christ.

Romans 6 is about *Living Above Sin.* It's a chapter that tells us not only why we should do so, but also how. It describes the power and the method. The heart of the chapter is really verse four:

> **4   Therefore we are buried with him by baptism into
> death: that like as Christ was raised up from the dead
> by the glory of the Father, even so we also should walk
> in newness of life.**

Paul's message is that what Christ has already done provides the
power for us to live above sin. Paul urges us to take advantage of
that power, so we will glorify God and produce much fruit.

The Purpose of the Crucifixion

First of all, our living above sin is the very purpose of the
crucifixion. Paul says in verses 1-3 that it is unthinkable ("**God
forbid!**") that we should go on living a sinful lifestyle after
receiving Christ. Why? Because when we were baptized, we **were
baptized into his death.** And the purpose of this was that **like as
Christ was raised up from the dead by the glory of the Father,
even so we also should walk in newness of life** (v.4).

Note two things about this purpose:

1. Christ died for sin to break its power in us

Verse 7 says, **For he that is dead is freed from sin.** Christ's death
freed him from the life that—even for the Son of God—was
vulnerable to sin (though he never yielded to temptation or
sinned). He broke sin's power at the cross.

2. Christ died unto sin so we could die to sin

The effect of what Christ did is that we can experience the
broken power of sin in our own lives. Christ died *unto sin* (v.10)
meaning he died having faithfully refused to sin in any way
throughout his whole life. His purpose in this was that we, by
being *in him*, might die *to* sin through him.

It was Christ's purpose in dying that we might be freed from
the power of sin and death. For us to be able to live new lives, lives

free of sin, its power over us had to be broken. We could not do it. Only Jesus could.

There were people in Paul's day who actually proposed that since God's grace was magnified—shown to be wonderfully magnificent—by the enormity of sin it overcame, believers shouldn't try to overcome sin, since it would just point up how gracious God is. That idea horrified Paul, and it ought to horrify every one of us. But really it's just an official statement of the philosophy that many people follow. They don't worry about their sins because in the back of their minds they count on God's wonderful forgiveness.

We would call it "taking God's grace for granted." To be more honest, it's presumptuous.

God's purpose is that we have a new kind of life, and for that new life we must first have a death to the old one, so it will no longer reign over us. This is why Jesus died.

The Power of the Resurrection

It's not so difficult to understand that God wants us to live above sin. What may dismay and discourage people, however, is repeated failure to do so. That's where the resurrection comes in at a practical level. For while the crucifixion of Christ points to God's purpose that we be freed from sin, the resurrection provides the power to do it. *The power of the resurrection* is the key to newness of life.

The key verses that inform us of this method of employing the power of the resurrection are 11 and 13. Those verses tell us two things we are to do:

1. Reckon on the facts of death and resurrection

Verse 11 says, **Likewise reckon ye yourselves to be dead indeed unto sin, but alive unto God through Jesus Christ our Lord.**

Two things happened to Jesus: he was crucified for sins and unto sin; and he was raised to conquer death and reign everlastingly in life. The Bible says that when we come into Christ by grace through faith, we are **baptized into his death.** Therefore we can *reckon* (count or consider) two things to be true: One, we are crucified with Christ unto sin; and two, we are raised with Christ unto new life and victory in his Lordship.

Here's where most people falter, many because they simply do not know about it: they don't reckon or count themselves dead to sin and they don't count themselves alive unto righteousness in Christ. They just keep trying in human strength, asking God to *help* them, but not relying on the already accomplished victory at the cross to be applied to their lives.

How would this work, this "reckoning" yourself to be dead to sin and alive to Christ? Face temptation in this way. Say to yourself, or say to God as you look into your own soul:

> I recognize I am being tempted to do something. My sin nature, or other people as the agents of sin, or perhaps Satan or one of his spirits, are placing thoughts of this sinful act or thought before my consciousness. The only reason it's a temptation at all is that my sinful self finds it appealing, because my sinful nature is perverted and base. But I am a new person in Christ. I am in Christ, because of God's grace through my acceptance of him by faith. I have been crucified with Christ unto sin. Lord, right now, I count myself dead to sin and I claim your victory over this temptation. I am alive in your Lordship. I claim the power of the resurrection to deny this temptation and live above this sin.

This is no magic incantation. But when you truly pray such things, say such things in your heart—or even out loud, if you can—to God, something happens. You get what God can do in and through you.

Of course, you cannot apply this kind of approach only to certain temptations and not to others. If you are otherwise living in surrender to various sins, you are not operating in the fullness of the Holy Spirit, not living under the Lordship of Christ, and you will probably find that your attempt to resist only certain temptations will fail utterly. Why? Because you are not genuinely seeking to live holy, but only to moderate your sinfulness.

Romans says, **Neither yield ye your members as instruments of unrighteousness unto sin: but yield yourselves unto God, as those that are alive from the dead, and your members as instruments of righteousness unto God.** We must surrender. Give up! Give up to God. In the release that comes when we abandon our wills and our control over our own lives and surrender to God's will and control, there will come the awesome experience of the influx of divine power. We will know the ability to live above sin.

No Christian is perfect. Some are truly holier in their living than others, but none perfect. So, is that any reason not to adopt this method of living that the Bible tells us to follow, just because we won't do it perfectly?

In baseball, players who consistently have a batting average of .350 are considered good hitters. A man with a .375 average for several seasons in a row would be considered a great hitter. Never mind that this means that out of every ten at bats he made an out more than six times. Never mind the fact that he may have struck out (and looked like a washerwoman doing it) more times than he got a hit. We think .375 is great!

Do people say, "I won't try to play baseball, or football, or tennis, or soccer, because I won't be perfect at it?" Does anyone ever apply this criteria to anything? Almost no one says this about anything. If something is worth doing, if it's worlds better than not doing it, then you do it.

Paul encourages us at two points:

1. Remember the bitter fruit of sin.

Romans 6:20-21 say: **When ye were the servants of sin, ye were free from righteousness. What fruit had ye then in those things whereof ye are now ashamed? For the end of those things is**

death. In a nutshell, without Christ there is no hope of being right before God and living above sin, and the results are always bitter and deadly. Sin comes to no good. Ever.

As the last verse of the chapter puts it: **For the wages of sin is death** (6:23). Paul is absolutely talking about dying and going out into eternity without hope, to exist apart from God forever.

The second encouragement from Paul is the positive side:

2. Repeat the better fruit of righteousness

Remind yourself how God blesses when you resist sin and do good, when you serve Christ, and follow the will of God. Has God ever disappointed you? The world is against you, troublesome circumstances take place, sin and sinners attack, and we constantly disappoint ourselves, but God is always good. He honors those who resist sin in the power of his Spirit and live above it.

As the last verse of the chapter also says: **But the gift of God is eternal life through Jesus Christ our Lord** (6:23).

Ultimately, we look forward to what verse five promises, that we will rise to everlasting lives free even of the presence of the sinful nature or temptation itself, forever. But until then, we are to live in newness of life. That's God's purpose. And in his power, we can begin to experience it, and grow in our likeness to Christ, who lived above all sin, always.

It may seem odd, this idea that death helps life, that something that dies enables something to live. But think about it.

In the world of medicine, many diseases can be prevented by vaccines. Vaccines are developed from the diseases they are meant to cure. There are two types of vaccines. One type is made by using various chemicals to kill live strains of the virus. Then the killed virus is injected into the body. The body recognizes the virus as an enemy, and quickly goes to work building antibodies against it, even though the virus is not doing anything, because it's dead. Voila, protection against the disease. Life set in motion by death.

Christ died for our sins. When we come into Christ, the Bible says that we are **baptized into his death.** This is far more than baptism in water. It means baptized in our spirits. The Holy Spirit comes into our lives and brings to pass a death to sin just like Christ's crucifixion, and he also brings to pass a resurrection to new life, through the entry of Christ himself, the risen Lord. Voila! We have the power of living above sin, in the crucified and risen Lord.

Here's a question for Christians: Are you living up to your potential in Christ? Do you want to rise to higher heights above temptation and sin? Then do what the Bible teaches: **Reckon ye also yourselves dead indeed unto sin, but alive unto God through Jesus Christ our Lord.**

Some readers of Romans may still not be convinced that salvation doesn't require at least *some* meritorious behavior on the part of the one seeking to be saved. Therefore, Paul continues in chapter 7 to talk about the folly of believing that trying to keep the law—even God's law—will help you on your way to heaven. As an added benefit, the upcoming chapter teaches Christians why they must live "by the Spirit" rather than "by the letter."

The Problem with the Law
Romans 7

Comedienne Rita Rudner once said the worst thing about flying is being seated behind some child who insists on playing peek-a-boo. She said, "Here's a game that has no ending. I want to tell him, 'Look, it's always going to be me!'"

In the first few chapters of Romans, Paul describes the effect of sin in much the same way: sin and death, sin and death. One leads to the other. It does so in every life. It has done so for millennia. It will do so until Christ comes again and the age ends and God separates sin from his creation forever.

In 1 Corinthians 15:56 Paul says clearly, "The strength of sin is the law." This gives us the key to the seventh chapter of Romans. Romans 7 is about the problem with the law. And the heart of that problem is really that if we insist on living by it, then like peek-a-boo it will always produce the same results: the face of sin. And sin always brings the ways of death.

The truths of Romans 7 are mostly summed up in v.6:

6   But now we are delivered from the law, that being dead wherein we were held; that we should serve in newness of spirit, and not in the oldness of the letter.

Let's be clear about what we're talking about when we say "the law." We're talking about trying to live by the law, the law of God, principles of moral and ethical living, and commandments of the worship and love of God.

The ancient Jews were given the law through Moses. They were invited to enter a covenant with God based on the law. They were to obey it. Throughout their history they discovered that individually and as a nation they were incapable of faithfully and perfectly following the law. Yet many Jews developed the idea that if they could just maintain a high level of obedience to it, they would earn eternal life. They maintained this belief even though they also went through the yearly ritual of offering sacrifices for sin. If they could earn a place in Abraham's Bosom, then what were the sacrifices for? Clearly, they had lost the sense of what the sacrifices meant or what they prophesied. Their dominant belief was that obeying the law merited them heaven.

This is a very common idea today, even among those who don't think the Bible's law is any more authoritative than any other. Still, people believe if they are "good" they'll go to heaven. They live by some "law," if only the law of their own consciences. But what do we all find by experience? We find that we can't even live by our own consciences perfectly.

The fact is, we sin. We disobey God. We break the law. We rebel. We slip. We miss the mark. We fail. We forget. We ignore it. We excuse ourselves for one reason or another. We blame others. We even blame God. But the bottom line is we all sin. Refer to Chapter 1 of this book and of Romans.

And this is really what the problem with the law is all about:

It ties us to death

First of all, the law ties us to death. We are born into a world where the absolute principles of God's righteousness are the guidelines for life—that's what it means to be born under the law. Paul wrote in Romans 3:19 that we are all "under the law," (so in Galatians 3:23 and 4:4), as we are born. And the first seven verses of Romans 7 describe this condition, the condition summarized in the words, **"the law hath dominion over a man"** (v.1). As long as the law has dominion over us, only one thing can happen, which Paul mentions in verse 5: **"When we were in the flesh, the motions of sins, which were *by the law*, did work in our members to bring forth fruit unto death."**

Paul illustrates the condition with the picture of a woman married to a man under Jewish law. He says she is **"bound by the law to her husband so long as he liveth"** (v.2). Consequently she is an adulteress if marries someone else. The only way this can change is if her husband dies. (By the way, it applies to men as well.) Then she is free. In a similar way, we are bound to the law, and if we rebel against it, we are sinners. And we all have rebelled, many times. And Romans 6:23 taught us clearly, **"The wages of sin is death."**

The law ties us to death. It can't do anything else! Over in Galatians 3:21 Paul admits that if there were a law that could have been given that would guarantee life, then the law would be about life. But there isn't. And so, the law ties us to death.

In our system of justice there are many kinds of crime and many varying punishments. A few things are considered to be so reprehensible, so damning, and so likely to be beyond reform, that someone convicted of those things must bear his or her guilt and even announce the fact of it wherever he goes for the rest of his life. Those who commit certain sexual crimes upon children are in this class. Wherever they live, they must register with police. In some places, there will be public notice made to neighbors about the person's past.

There is debate about this law, not because sexual predators are easily reformed—because they aren't—but because of the principle of paying one's debt to society. If one is never free of implied guilt and accusation as long as he lives, wouldn't it be better to be locked up?

This is something like the miserable quandary that we all face under the law. It ties us to the guilt of our past sin, and to the inevitability of future sin, by its very nature. As long as we are under the law, we are tied to death.

It finds us guilty

Just exactly why the law ties us to death is that the law finds us guilty. Its very purpose is to define sin and identify sinners.

In verses 7-13, Paul says that the law is a good thing, but it's function is to tell us bad news: **"I had not known sin, but by the law: for I had not known lust, except the law had said, Thou shalt not covet."** What happens is that sin **takes occasion by the commandment** to produce sin in us. The Twentieth Century New Testament translates that verse, "Sin took advantage of the commandment to arouse in me every form of covetousness."

When God told Adam and Eve not to eat of the tree in the middle of the garden, that was a good thing. That one law, the only one they had, made clear to them what was not allowed. There was nothing unclear about the law, and they understood the purpose of it perfectly. But sin came along in the temptation of Satan, and lured Eve into desiring the very thing God's one and only law had prohibited.

That's how the law ties us to death: it finds us guilty by defining what is wrong, which gives sin an opportunity to lure us into disobedience.

"The law is spiritual," writes Paul (v.14). What's wrong is sin, and sin makes use of the law to create wrong desires in our hearts. So the law finds us guilty at every turn.

Out on a stretch of interstate highway in one state the speed limit was recently lowered to 60 m.p.h. The rationale was to reduce accidents on a busy corridor between two major cities. Before that, the limit was 65. But years before that, it was 55.

Suppose you're driving along that stretch, and you miss the sign that says 55, and you're doing 60. Or what if it drops to 45 in a work zone that you don't notice. You could be apprehended, and rightly so. Why? Because that's the law. It doesn't matter that the law used to be 65, or that in some states a stretch like that might be 70. This is here, this is now, and this stretch has a posted speed limit. It's the law. And that law defines what is illegal to do.

That's what God's law does. Man's laws sometimes change, but God's law does not. And it defines sin with absoluteness. And since all of us are born *in sin*—meaning, under its influence and control—the law therefore inevitably finds us to be sinners.

That's the problem with the law! And one more thing:

It leaves us short

The law leaves us short. It doesn't enable us to do good. It only tells us what bad is.

Many people have found a sort of comfort in reading in

Romans 7:15 and the verses following. They feel better hearing that Paul had trouble doing what he knew to be right, and avoiding what he knew to be wrong. Now, Paul certainly does not mean to say that he is a bad example of Christian life. But he does admit to the struggle that all of us have with temptation.

He writes: **"What I would, that do I not; but what I hate, that do I"** (7:15) In English more like what we would speak, 'What I want to do that's good, I don't do. Instead, I do the things I realize are wrong.' Or even, 'I can't help doing wrong!'

And he comes to this powerful conclusion: **"It is no more I that do it, but sin that dwelleth in me"** (v.17). Paul doesn't specifically talk about the two natures—fleshly and spiritual—that are in Christians, but that's what he's referring to here. And he *is* talking about Christians. Because shortly he says, **"I delight in the law of God after the inward man"** (v.22). He's talking about the problem that even Christians have with keeping the old sinful self down, and living up to the righteousness of God. We have two natures: one of them, the new nature, names Jesus Lord and wants to serve God. But the other, the old sin nature, is still there and wants to do "its own thing." That's who's in control when you sin: your old nature.

If even Christians have a problem with this old nature of sin, those who have yet to come to Christ have multiplied more problems. Because without Christ, there is no new nature, no power of God to overcome sin.

So Paul says it boils down to this: **"I find a law, that, when I would do good, evil is present with me ...[a] law in my members, warring against the law of my mind, and bringing me into captivity to the law of sin"** (vv.21,23). Just as we said earlier: sin and death. Sin and death.

When we want to do good, sin fights us deep inside. And all too often it wins. In fact, unless something interrupts this process of death in us, sin will win for good. And Paul expresses this plaintive cry of the human heart: **"O wretched man that I am! Who shall deliver me from the body of this death?"** (v.24). It is this body, this flesh, that has been infected and totally affected by sin. As long as we are in it, sin will be a problem for us. So what is the answer?

"I thank God through Jesus Christ our Lord" (v.25). This is the answer! Christ is the *only* answer! Only through Jesus Christ will the power of sin be broken, the reign of sin be ended, and slavery to the law obliterated.

Jesus has come and died for sin as a sinless Savior, so that the law might be fulfilled in him, and we might be freed from it. Paul gave the solution in verse 4: **"Ye are become dead to the law by the body of Christ; that ye should be married to another, even to him who is raised from the dead, that we should bring forth fruit unto God."**

The principle of spiritual life this chapter teaches us is that we are to recognize the presence of the sin nature in us, realize that in Christ we have received the power of being crucified to it, and then to count ourselves dead to the flesh every day, every moment and hour of every day. Then we are to realize we have a new nature from God, count ourselves alive unto Christ, and proclaim him Lord in our hearts every moment of every hour, every day. That way, we will escape the *problem with the law.* We will be living *under grace.*

The problem with the law is not *what* it requires. What it requires is holiness to God. That's as it should be. The problem with the law is that it doesn't provide what we need to obey it. What we need, then, and what God does, is not to change his own standards of holiness. He simply puts us in a new position of life: grace. And he gives us a new power for living: Jesus Christ. That's how he solves *the problem with the law.*

How, then, is this new power for living, which is in fact Jesus Christ himself, given to us? That's the subject to which Paul turns in Romans 8.

The Mission of the Spirit of Christ
Romans 8

The idea of "mission" is very important. Businesses have picked up on it in the past few generations, and more and more we run into "mission statements" in companies and corporations—and churches. Organizations come up with these statements to help them define what they're here for.

Jesus knew what he was here for. His mission statement was, "The Son of Man is come to seek and save that which is lost." And just before he left the world he told his disciples he would send someone to encourage us and to be with us. And that someone is the Holy Spirit. His mission is to abide with us forever (Jn.14:16), teach us everything we need to know (1 Jn. 2:27), and reveal Christ unto us (Jn.16:26).

There are other places the Bible teaches us about the mission of the Holy Spirit in more detail. One of those is Romans 8. In this chapter Paul is concerned with our discovering the great power of God that the Holy Spirit brings, and in our allowing him to do his work in us. The heart of that chapter might be considered to be verses 8-10, which say:

8 **So then they that are in the flesh cannot please God.**
9 **But ye are not in the flesh, but in the Spirit, if so be that the Spirit of God dwell in you. Now if any man have not the Spirit of Christ, he is none of his.**
10 **And if Christ be in you, the body is dead because of sin; but the Spirit is life because of righteousness.**

The Bible teaches us that the Spirit of God, the Holy Spirit, is the Spirit of Jesus himself. We can almost "mix and match" those titles and whatever we come up with we will still have the same being: God. The Holy Spirit is the Spirit of Christ. That's how Jesus can be at the right hand of the throne of the Father in heaven and be in our hearts and lives individually at the same time: the Holy Spirit makes Jesus real in our lives. That's his main mission.

But to break it down as Paul does is helpful, because we see what specific things God is trying to accomplish in us while we are in this world.

If there were a mission statement about the Spirit of Christ in us, it might be this: The mission of the Spirit of Christ is to bring us victory in life, power in sonship, confidence and communication, and to finish the saving work of God.

Let's take that a quarter at a time. First quarter:

Victory in Life

The Spirit's mission is to bring us victory in life. He brings life itself, because he is life, and he brings us victory because he is in us to conquer our sin nature and empower us against temptation and for every challenge.

The chapter begins with the wonderful announcement that those who are in Christ Jesus (which results in his being in us) have **no condemnation** (v.1), as we now **walk after the Spirit.** That means we have a different kind of life, and have a right relationship with God. It says we have been **freed** from the **law of sin and death** (v.2), which is the trap we can't get out of on our own through good works.

And the practical value of this is that now that the Spirit is in us, he is here to fulfill the **righteousness of the law** (v.4) in us, which he does by simply being in us. Jesus fulfilled the law, and if he is in us, as a part of us, we benefit from his perfection. As someone said, God looks at us, and sees Jesus Christ.

Not only that, but the Spirit also gives us the ability to think with the mind of Christ, and to **mind** (vv.6-7) the things of God. So we can sense what God is saying to us, begin to think spiritually instead of in a worldly way, and know the will of God. And not only know it, but also begin to do it, in the power of the Spirit.

The result is that **to be spiritually minded is life and peace** (v.6). This is what brings us victory in life—being spiritually minded. Because what we are before we receive Christ is **carnally minded** (v.6), which means "fleshly." And verse 8 says, "**they that**

are in the flesh cannot please God."

But they who are spiritually minded do please God, because they are responding to the Spirit of Christ in them, and as they obey they are depending on that same Spirit for the power to resist temptation and meet every challenge.

The key to victory in life is first to know Christ personally, and second to trust him and surrender to him daily, thinking spiritually, walking spiritually, acting spiritually. When we do that, we overcome, instead of being overwhelmed.

Second quarter:

Power in Sonship

The mission of the Spirit of Christ in us is also to bring power in our sonship to God.

In most languages there is simply a choice to be made between genders, and women will have to be content to accept the fact that the Bible calls us the "sons" of God without any difference between men and women, boys and girls. Some modern translations render the Greek word as "children," and there's no reason not to do so in this context except that Paul parallels our relationship with God to that of Jesus Christ. The concept in these verses is simply that God has adopted us into his family by the saving work of Jesus Christ, and we become sons of God because we are part of him who is *the* Son of God.

This comes about when we receive Jesus personally. And v.9 says, **"Now if any man have not the Spirit of Christ, he is none of his."** This is a very important verse in the entire Bible. If Jesus Christ by his Spirit is not in you, you are not one of his: you are not a child of God; you are not saved. Either he is in you and you *have* him, or he is not and you don't. And if he is, you will know it. If you have never known it, always doubted it, or just learned about it and realize there is something you've missed, you need to hear this word, so listen carefully: Jesus must be in you by the Spirit for you to be a saved child of God. You will not have God's victory in life, not have peace with God, and will not go to heaven if you do not have Jesus Christ.

How do you "get" the Spirit of Jesus Christ? You receive him. You ask him into your heart and life, in an act of repentance and personal trust in him. You surrender your life to him. It's personal. It's conscious. It's intentional. It's a decision you make, and must make for yourself, if you want to have forgiveness and eternal life.

Paul writes that **if Christ be in you, the body is dead because of sin; but the Spirit is life because of righteousness** (v.10). Without Christ, only the first part of that verse is true: you are dead in sins. But with Christ, you are alive in him, so that when the body dies, you will go on, in the presence of the Lord forever.

Verse 11 goes on to promise that the saved will be raised to live with Christ forever, again because the Spirit of Christ is in you.

Consequently, verses 12-17 tell us that we ought to live like sons of God, like children of God, not in bondage to fear, but in confidence of our belonging specially to God. We are **heirs of God, and joint-heirs with Christ** (v.17), and if we **suffer with him,** it is only that we may also be **glorified** with him.

This was God's plan from the beginning, that we should be his sons and daughters, acting in power, experiencing his presence, knowing we belong to him, knowing he is our heavenly Father. The word used in v.15 for "father" is the Aramaic *abba*, the equivalent of our English "daddy." The relationship between a Christian and God is to be intimate, personal, warm, and loving. God will be this way to us. Will we be this way toward God?

Third quarter:

Confidence and Communication

The Spirit of Christ is in us to bring confidence and communication with God.

Verses 18-25 are all about the hope we have in Christ, hope of **the glory which shall be revealed in us** (v.18), hope for the **glorious liberty of the children of God** (v.21). These are descriptions of what our lives will be like in eternity, far more glorious than these bodies, and freed from any sin or limitation.

Paul talks about how we **groan** while we are **waiting** for all this to happen (v.23), and in fact he pictures the entire creation groaning, urgent to be out from under the weight of sin's curse and condemnation. We make it through by the **hope** the Spirit gives us (vv.24-25). We are **saved** by that hope (v.24). We don't see heaven yet, but the Spirit of God makes us certain of it and certain of our going there, because we are certain he is in us, bearing **witness with our spirit, that we are the children of God** (v.16).

And while we wait, we also communicate with God, express our frustrations and our hopes, our dreams and our burdens, and the Spirit also helps us in that communication. This is prayer. The Spirit of God knows not only God, which he is, but also knows us as well, and helps us to pray effectively.

Let's risk an illustration from computer science—quickly outdated by the pace of computer development. The computer chip maker Intel has used a logo that it contracts with computer builders to be emblazoned on every computer that contains one of their processors. It's a little swirl and the words "Intel inside." When you see that, you know you have a genuine Intel chip—like the Pentium—inside the computer.

Well, the Christian has *God inside.* There is an inner witness to our being saved.

There are many Bible verses that make the case for assurance of our salvation, but this inward knowledge of God by his Spirit gives us confidence in our being heaven-bound. How wonderful to have God *inside,* where we need confidence and hope!

And the final quarter:

To Finish the Saving Work of God
The Holy Spirit of Christ is in us to finish the saving work of God.

In one way, the work of salvation was done at Calvary and in the open tomb. Jesus said, "It is finished." In the eternal sense, the completed work of Christ is undeniable.

There is another sense to God's working, and that's the way he begins a good work in us (Phil.2:6), and then continues to perform it unto the day of Christ Jesus. It's what Paul calls being changed from glory unto glory (2 Cor.3:18). Here in Romans he describes the transformation in these steps: foreknowledge, predestination, calling, justification, glorification (vv.29-30). From timeless eternity when God knew us before we were, to the moment he called us to follow Christ, to the steps of our spiritual growth, and finally to the time of our becoming like Jesus in glory, God is at work to complete this creation in us.

In part, that's why we know we have security in salvation. God finishes what he starts, and he started a good work in us. No one is going to thwart him in that, not Satan, not our enemies, not sin, not even you yourself. God has you in his hands.

Everything that happens to us happens in order to work out the details of that plan. That's what Romans 8:28 says. It assures us that the Spirit of God is able to take anything that comes our way and weave it into the tapestry of God's plan for our lives, a plan to bless us, here and hereafter. In an even more amazing way discussed to some extent in Romans 9, God sovereignly plans the entire pilgrimage.

Thinking about all this, Paul launches into a doxology, praising God for his powerful and secure love, saying **we are more than conquerors through him that loved us** (v.37), and that nothing **shall be able to separate us from the love of God, which is in Christ Jesus our Lord** (v.39).

All this is the mission of the Spirit of Christ: to make us the children of God and take us every step of the way until we meet the Lord face to face, and live eternally with him.

Various Christian denominations have mission ventures in many countries of the world. Some of these countries welcome missionaries, because they often do more than establish churches and win converts. They help in many other ways like medicine, relief, education, or development. But other countries do not welcome missionaries so much. They are suspicious of Christians' motives. The going is harder for missionaries when they are fought, resisted, or restricted.

The same is true in us. The Spirit of Christ has a mission. If you're a Christian, you invited him to come perform that mission. So welcome him every day, obey his leading, respond to his voice, move with his moving, so he can make you a victor, bring you life and hope, and finish the work he started when you first said, "Jesus is Lord."

When Paul first began writing details about the vital subject of God's grace, he taught that grace is received by faith. In chapter 9, Paul goes into greater detail about this faith, which is the means by which we receive or lay hold of God's grace and everything God offers through it.

The Merciful Gift of Faith

Romans 9

It is one of the more glorious and wonderful truths of the scripture that God has not left anything to accident. When we speak of a sovereign God, this is one of the things we must talk about.

It is especially important that when we talk about God's offer of eternal life to man—what we call salvation—we understand that God has provided for every element of that salvation, from the sacrifice for sins in Jesus Christ, to the resurrection for new life, to the worldwide spread of the gospel message that gives us a chance to respond. Not only this, but God has also provided the means for us to respond to him. Because if it were left up to us, we could not and would not turn to God.

The Bible makes it clear that "all our righteousnesses are as filthy rags" (Is.64:6), and that "there is none righteous, no not one" (Ps.14:1-3,53:1-3). Paul wrote with deliberate clarity, "There is none that seeketh after God" (Rom.3:11), and later in Corinthians, "The natural man receiveth not the things of the Spirit" (1 Cor.2:14). We could look at many more scriptures that make it clear that if left up to man, he will not turn to God. Turning to God is a work of the Spirit in our hearts. Repentance is a work of God's grace. Jesus said, "No man can come to me except the Father who sent me draw him" (Jn.6:44).

We may wonder how this could be, since many of us remember being interested in spiritual things, in seeking something to fulfill our lives, in searching for God. But this is exactly what the Bible teaches us: that this sort of interest and urgency is the result of God's working in our hearts, for without it, we would run away from God, not come to him.

So if God does this work of grace in our hearts, how do we respond to him? The Bible calls the right response "faith." But where does faith come from? The scripture is again clear: faith, too, is a work of God. It comes from God. It is a response in our hearts to the word of God (Rom.10:17). In short, faith is a merciful gift of God. For if God did not give us faith, we would have none.

Some of the more well known salvation "formulas" in the Bible verify this. Ephesians 2:8: "For by grace are you saved through faith, and *that* not of yourselves, it is the gift of God." *That* refers to faith itself.

Romans 9 is about this merciful gift of faith. Romans 9-11 is usually taken as a description of God's wonderful plan to choose and call a people unto himself. Chapter 9 tells how he sovereignly moves in history to call a people unto himself, and how faith is the key element in their response.

The heart of chapter 9 is v.16:

So then it is not of him that willeth, nor of him that runneth, but of God that sheweth mercy.

The word "it" in this verse refers to the calling of God mentioned in verse 11. God calls people to belong to him. And this calling is not about what *we* want (**not of him that willeth**), or about what we try to do to earn God's favor and salvation (**nor of him that runneth**), but simply a matter of God's sovereign decision to have mercy (**but of God that sheweth mercy**).

And the heart of this mercy from God is in the gift of faith, the ability to believe in Christ. See what this chapter teaches us about this merciful gift of faith:

It Brings Us Salvation

First, God's merciful gift of faith brings us salvation. It's the only response that will open the door and let us receive the saving gift of God in Christ.

Verses 1-10 make it abundantly clear that it isn't belonging to a church or to a certain "people" that saves us, but believing in Jesus. Paul grieves for his fellow Israelites, who after all were the ones to receive the law and to have the prophets of God minister in their midst, and who were the people out of which the Messiah, Jesus, actually came (vv.3-5). But they didn't, as a nation, receive him. True, the first church was entirely Jewish, and the first several thousand believers were Jews. But nationally, Israel rejected Jesus.

Did that mean God's word was ineffective, because few of them wound up believing in their own Messiah? No. Because, as Paul says, **They are not all Israel, which are of Israel** (v.6). By this he means not everyone who is of the *nation* Israel is one of the spiritual descendants of Israel the *man,* who was the child of Abraham by promise. Abraham and Sarah could not have a child, but then God gave them one by miracle—Isaac. He told them of his plan, and the Bible says "Abraham believed God." Isaac is the symbol of being born into the family of God by faith. They are not all children of God by faith who are children of godly people by birth. Being born into a Christian family, or joining a Christian church, doesn't make you a child of God. Children are born to God through faith.

So the gift of faith is what brings us salvation, not joining anything, or being baptized, or having Christian parents, or *anything else!*

We should have no problem in recognizing that our placing our faith in Jesus is ultimately a gift from God and not something we do all on our own. It arises out of our deepest hearts, and expresses our most personal longing. Nobody is forcing us to believe on Jesus. But it was simply God who supernaturally enabled us to feel this way. Without his merciful gift, sin would get the better of us all, and we would not turn to him.

It Comes By His Plan

So faith is a merciful gift of God, that brings us salvation. And as such, it also comes by his plan. In other words, it isn't our plan, but his. He chooses *us*, and only in response, by the faith he gives us, do we choose *him.*

Paul begins telling us, in verse 10, of the history of Rebecca and Isaac. Of their two children, Jacob and Esau, God chose one to bless by making him the father of the nation through whom would come the law, the prophets, and eventually the Messiah. That was Jacob. The other son God chose *not* to so bless. This is the real sense of **"Jacob I loved, but Esau I hated"** (v.13). It does not mean God hated him as people often say about one another. That's an attitude of malice and spite that God knows nothing of.

Paul says this matter of choice is entirely up to God, and that he has the perfect right to have compassion on some, and not on others (v.15). As an example, he chose to harden the Egyptian Pharaoh to the entreaties of Moses, so that his plan would be worked out for the people of his choice, the Hebrews.

Verse 18 twice uses the word **will: "Therefore hath he mercy on whom he *will* [have mercy], and whom he *will* he hardeneth."** The entire matter is one of God's choice, God's plan.

For centuries, people have debated this matter of God's choosing a people to save. Many are incensed at the idea that God would leave anybody out of his plan to save. There are a couple of ways to look at this:

- First, for God to choose anyone is totally his prerogative—he doesn't have to save anyone. We are the ones who left God, who sinned, and who rebel against him. Nothing is required for justice but that those who have sinned be allowed to suffer its consequence, which is death and hell. That God chooses to save anyone at all is merciful, and we should be thankful for it.
- Second, Jesus himself said, "All that the Father giveth to me will come to me, and him that cometh to me I will in no wise cast out" (John 6:37). If you come to Jesus asking for salvation, you should have no fear that you may be denied. The matter of God's choice is hardly relevant at all to our actual experience of the gospel. We needn't worry ourselves about whom God has chosen, and whom he may not have. If you come to Jesus, you will be welcomed into the family of God.

The very concern that some feel about whether or not they could be saved is an indication that God may be working on their hearts to draw them to him. Our worry should be with responding rightly to God, not figuring out the intricacies of the divine mystery of his plan.

But we need to probe this idea a bit further, just so we are clear on where faith comes from and who is to be the focus of all this:

It Glorifies God's Mercy

The gift of faith glorifies God's divine mercy. We have called it a merciful gift. And it is just this mercy that is to be glorified. Our experiencing faith, faith placed in Christ, points up—glorifies—the fact that God is merciful.

Mercy and grace are often used together. There is a slight difference. Grace is God's giving us what we do not deserve. Mercy is his not giving us what we *do* deserve. That God should save anyone is merciful. Every person who has placed his faith in Christ should glorify God for his mercy.

Verses 19-21 state a very important Bible truth, that no one has any business questioning the right of God to deal with his creation as he sees fit, or to conclude that God is unjust for doing one thing or another. **O man, who art thou that repliest against God?**

Verse 21 pictures God as a potter, working with a lump of clay, who first fashions a piece for an honorable use, and then something for a less honorable use. For instance, the first is a prized vase and the second is a chamber pot. Or one is a cruse to hold oil, another a target for children to use while practicing their slingshots. The potter has the perfect right to design both pieces.

Paul carries the illustration further to make certain we understand that we have no right to indict God with unfairness. And then he tells us that such discussion misses the point, anyway, because what is really in focus is God's mercy. That any at all are saved glorifies God in his mercy.

He says, **in the place where it was said unto them, Ye are not my people, there shall they be called the children of the living God** (v.26). And verse 29 virtually puts it in bold and italics: *Except the Lord of Sabaoth had left us a seed, we had been as Sodoma, and*

been made as Gomorrha. This is how the Jew should see it—that
God has continued to provide that a remnant of Jews shall come
to their Messiah.

This is how we Gentiles should see it, as well: that we are
floating down the river toward an immense waterfall and certain
death, but God plucks persons out of the rushing waters and
places us on heaven's shores; that we are falling from a precipice
to the rocks below, but that God bears us up on angel's wings and
sets us down in green pastures of salvation; that we are in the path
of a deadly stampede, but that God lifts us out at the last second.

Who are we to presume that we could, if we debated God
about it, understand the intricacies of his plan and his reasoning?
Our place is to glorify God for his mercy.

It Leaves Us Responsible

We have seen that God's merciful gift of faith brings us
salvation; and it comes by his plan and choosing alone; and it
glorifies his mercy. But God's merciful gift of faith also leaves us
responsible. The Bible truth that God is sovereign, chooses a
people, and has mercy on whom he will, doesn't change the fact
that we are accountable for our response to Christ. The gospel
contains nothing that asks us to understand God's inscrutable
ways. It simply tells us we're sinners in need of salvation, and
offers us Jesus Christ as God's Savior. He died for our sins and rose
again to bring us eternal life. How will you respond to him? That's
the only relevant question for one who has not yet received Christ.

After all Paul's discussion of God's choice, his plan, his mercy
on some and his hardening others, he ends this chapter by saying
clearly that we are responsible for placing our faith in Christ and
not rejecting him for some other hope—even the hope that there
is no eternal justice.

In verse 30 Paul says that the Gentiles **have attained to
righteousness, even the righteousness which is of faith**, but that
Israel had not attained this righteousness. Here, "righteousness"
is another word for being saved—it means being made right with

God, which is what salvation is.

And how did this happen? It happened because Israel, the Jews, **sought it not by faith, but as it were by the works of the law** (v.31). They tried to earn it. But the Gentiles responded to the gospel, placed their faith in Christ alone, and were saved.

Paul's illustration is of Christ as a stumbling stone, a **rock of offence** (v.33), which some stumble over, and others climb up on for salvation. We are responsible for whether we take offense at the message of the gospel, or take it to heart and obey it.

Let God understand how election and choice and his plan work. We are responsible for turning to Christ through faith, for believing him to be the Son of God, for believing he died for our sins, for believing he rose from the grave, and for trusting him to save us when we call on his name. If we place our faith in him, we have God to thank for it. But if we reject him, we have no one to blame but ourselves.

So what will you do with Jesus?

The bottom line for us, then, is what our response will be. In fact, the closing phrase of chapter 9 leaves the reader with the statement and holy enticement: **"whosoever believeth on him shall not be ashamed."** The words are Paul's invitation to believe the gospel of Jesus Christ, to make the all important decision to trust him.

There is no one around us who can make the decision for us. There is no one who will force us to receive Christ, to believe on him. There is no membership in any church, no belonging to any family, no connection to any dear saint, no possession of a Bible, no record of church attendance, no friendliness toward Christians, churches, preachers, or religion in general, no sincerity about spirituality in general, no good intentions, and no record of good deeds, that will make any difference at all to God. He has laid out the way of salvation, and it is placing personal faith in Jesus Christ, receiving him as Lord of our lives, that brings us salvation. Nothing else.

When Jesus was tried before Roman authorities, the procurator Pontius Pilate ironically expressed well for every one of us the choice we must make. When the Jews chose to have Barabbas released from custody instead of Jesus, Pilate said, "What then shall I do then with Jesus, who is called Christ?"

What indeed?

An Offer We Can't Refuse

Romans 10

One of the classic lines from the movie *The Godfather* was spoken by the godfather himself, Marlon Brando. In a particularly menacing threat he told someone, "I'm going to make him an offer he can't refuse." He meant if the offer was refused, the consequences were dire.

We can always refuse any offer. But sometimes the consequences are disastrous. Sometimes the offer may come from someone who doesn't mean us any good. But sometimes it comes from God. He, too, makes us a wonderful offer—salvation, a new birth, eternal life. And it's an offer that if we refuse, we are choosing dire consequences.

The question is why would we refuse an offer for something we most desperately need? Some refuse salvation because they are skeptical about the Bible, religious talk, churches, the whole nine yards. Some turn away from the gospel—the good news of salvation—because they think there is another way to be saved, one that is less demanding than the command to name Jesus Lord of your life. Some say "no" not intending to refuse always, just putting it off until they feel ready. Some have arguments with theology and the Bible. Some have been offended by various Christians they know. There are many reasons.

But all of them will seem so terribly inadequate when the dire consequences of not being saved come to pass. When that happens, people will wish they had taken the offer we can't refuse.

Romans 10 is about this tremendous offer that God will save us through Jesus Christ. The heart of that chapter is verses 9-10:

9 **That if thou shalt confess with thy mouth the Lord Jesus, and shalt believe in thine heart that God hath raised him from the dead, thou shalt be saved.**

10 **For with the heart man believeth unto righteousness; and with the mouth confession is made unto salvation.**

The gospel is the message that God has sent himself in the person of Jesus Christ, to save us from eternal condemnation, by taking our penalty for us on the cross. By rising from the dead, he becomes an ever-living Savior. If we repent of sin and receive him, we will be forgiven and have eternal life.

This is the offer we can't refuse. We simply cannot afford to say "no." Why?

Salvation by Faith

First, because it's an offer of salvation by faith. It doesn't come any easier than that. Most people think salvation (if they believe they need it at all) is by some form of works. They try all their lives to be good, to merit a reward. Or they don't especially try, they just hold out hope that they will be judged to have been good enough, just on the basis of their natural merits.

Paul talks about that approach to living in Romans 10:1-10.In verse 1 he says he prays his own countrymen will be saved, but says they're on the wrong track, since they're **going about to establish their own righteousness** (v.3). He explains that Moses said of the law, **"The man which doeth those things shall live by them"** (v.5). The context and the verb tense Paul uses make it clear that he means **doeth** with no exception—lives perfectly. Obviously no one has done or can do that.

God, however, has made us an offer we can't afford to refuse: **That if thou shalt confess with thy mouth the Lord Jesus, and shalt believe in thine heart that God hath raised him from the dead, thou shalt be saved** (v.9). There it is: salvation by faith, not by works. **For with the heart man believeth unto righteousness; and with the mouth confession is made unto salvation** (v.10). Salvation is a matter of placing your faith in Jesus Christ, not in your own goodness or works.

Why has God chosen to make faith the avenue of salvation? Because if it were by works, we could give the credit to ourselves. Because it's by faith, the credit goes to God.

Verses 6-7 are a loose quote from Deuteronomy 30:12-13, where

Moses waxes poetic telling the Israelites they don't need to go far and wide or reach to heaven to find God or discover his will—God has laid it out before them in his revelation. Paul says in a similar way salvation isn't about our finding God, or convincing him to come to us. It's about God's already having come to us in Jesus Christ. All we have to do is receive him by faith.

Eternal Life Free

Not only is salvation by faith, but also because it is, eternal life is free. That's the second reason salvation is an offer we just can't refuse.

In Romans 10:11-15, the Bible says God is **rich unto all that call upon him. For whosoever shall call upon the name of the Lord shall be saved** (vv.12-13). It's free for the asking.

This free gift comes about as the result of a chain of events described in 14-15: We can believe because we have now heard. We heard because someone preached or proclaimed Christ to us. That person or persons were sent by God. And **How beautiful are the feet of them that preach the gospel of peace!** (v.15).

Eternal life is free for the asking. When we hear the gospel, that's our chance, our opportunity to take the gift that keeps on giving—really and truly—keeps on giving for eternity!

We live in a skeptical age. There are many people who believe nothing is free. We get offers on the phone by people who say, "I'm not selling you anything," and we know they are. We have internet access that says "totally free," but we know the price is really our privacy. We see ads that proclaim this or that is free with the purchase of *whatever,* and we know they have simply covered the cost of the giveaway in the other thing they're selling. It's not that there aren't any good deals out there—there are. It's just that seldom does anything really cost absolutely nothing.

So we hear the Bible calling salvation "the free gift" (Romans 5:15), and preachers saying, "Just believe on Jesus, and the gift is yours," and it sounds too good to be true. Is it?

Well, admittedly salvation cost God something. It cost God the life of Jesus Christ, in an ignominious and shameful death in which the sin of the world was placed on Christ and he bore it to the cross. We cannot imagine what that was like for the sinless Jesus.

In addition to that, in order to receive the free gift you must give up your life—that's true. You must give your very self to Christ. Looked at that way, it seems that salvation costs you your life, but salvation isn't a matter of giving up anything, but of exchanging it for something better. In essence, in receiving salvation, you give up what you cannot keep, for something you cannot lose.

Consider the man who is floating down a rushing river, grasping at logs that are rushing along beside him, trying vainly to swim against the current, or trying to find a foothold where there is none. If a life preserver were thrown to him, he would have to stop trying to get a foothold, leave trying to reach that log, and cease trying to swim. But ask him if he thinks grabbing hold of the life preserver "costs" him anything. He will tell you no, in no uncertain terms. Grabbing hold will save him, and the offer is something he can't refuse.

Salvation is by faith. It doesn't cost anything. All we must do is abandon all our hopeless hopes, our futile trying, and let Jesus Christ save us instead.

What makes salvation an offer you can't refuse is that it's by the simple means of faith, and that it's free for your asking. But what makes it an offer you must not dare to refuse is that the alternative is not to be desired under any circumstances:

Believe or Perish

Simply put, we must receive salvation, free and by faith, or we will pay for our own sins, eternally. Believe or perish.

This is what makes the gospel, the good news, so good: the bad news is so very bad.

In vv.16-21 Paul tearfully deals with the stubbornness of his own people, the Jews, to believe in their Messiah, Jesus Christ. He says, **they have not all obeyed the gospel** (v.16), not because they have not heard, because they have (v.18). By the time Paul wrote these words, the gospel had traveled to most of the known world and no nation was unaware of the Jews and their Bible and its prophecies of a messiah. This word had been carried by dispersed Jews throughout the entire world.

It wasn't that they didn't know, but that they didn't believe. God even said he would have non-Jews believe enthusiastically in the Messiah, so the Jews would be motivated by **jealousy** (v.19) to believe. For all that, God says **All day long I have stretched forth my hands unto a disobedient and gainsaying people** (v.21). The word "gainsaying" means argumentative. The Jews contradicted and argued with the plain truth in front of them of God's salvation. The most recent and the ultimate example of this denial of truth was in their refusal to believe that Jesus was God's Messiah.

There is only one result of this disbelief: to perish eternally. That's why Paul was so distressed about his own countrymen's lack of faith. He knew the consequences: believe or perish.

Jesus himself said, "He who believes on me is not condemned, but he who believes not is condemned already, because he has not believed in the name of the only begotten Son of God" (Jn.3:18). In the most memorable verse in the Bible, John 3:16, Jesus gave the wonderful news of his sacrifice for us, including a reminder of the consequences of not believing: "For God so loved the world that he gave his only begotten Son, that whosoever believeth in him should not *perish*, but have everlasting life."

Apparently, many people simply don't believe it is this serious, that the consequences of not becoming a believer in Jesus Christ could possibly be that dire. Many people don't believe in heaven and hell and think that it doesn't matter. Even among those who do suspect strongly the Bible may be true, many think there will always be time to take care of eternal matters *later*.

In February, 2001, racing fans watched the Daytona 500 as Dale Earnhardt was involved in a violent crash. Crews surrounded the car, the red flag went out, and the crowd that ordinarily would have cheered without reservation for the winner instead looked on in shock. Dale Earnhardt, whom many fans would say in the days to come "was" NASCAR, was cut out of his harness and rushed to the hospital, where he died.

Even the non-racing fans were a bit stunned. A church leader with a group in a pizza parlor, watching the events on a big-screen TV, said, "I just hope he was ready."

We never know what a moment will bring. People who die in auto crashes, on or off a track, don't go out driving thinking they will die that day. People who die of heart attacks seldom expect to. People who are shot in robberies, fall from construction scaffolds, get hit by cars, or just discover deadly diseases have ravaged them, have not sat down and calendared these events. It doesn't just happen to famous people or 'someone else.' The mortality rate is the same in every state: one per person.

Jesus was approached by people who were aghast at the death met by some Galilean Jews who had been killed by Romans and their blood mingled with sacrifices—adding supreme insult to injury. People thought, "How awful, how terrible." But Jesus asked if they thought these people were worse than anyone else, that their case was somehow distant and remote. "I tell you nay," he said, "but except ye repent, ye shall all likewise perish."

We are shocked at the sudden deaths of famous people, sports idols, political figures, entertainers, high school football players, people in their prime, but today or tomorrow the world around you right now may be saying of you, "I hope he was ready. I hope she was prepared to meet God."

Paul quotes Isaiah 65:2 where God says, **all day long I have stretched forth my hands.** God reaches out to us and urges us to come to him. Salvation is an offer you can't refuse—cannot afford to turn down. You mustn't! It's free; it's by simple faith; it's eternal life, for goodness sake—why would you refuse?

Who Are God's People?

Romans 11

Many of the wars of this world have been fought over conflicting claims of just who God's people are. Certainly the land now called Israel, a bridge connecting three continents, has been the site of endless such controversy. Both Jews and Arabs claim to be God's chosen people.

The argument is not limited to Jews and Arabs, or even Christians, however. Many groups in the world believe they are God's special people. Many religions have an element of exclusiveness, a claim to a unique standing in God's eyes.

We believe the Bible answers this question. While Christians realize that many people don't accept the Bible as their source of authority, we believe history, testimony, and most of all Jesus Christ, have demonstrated that the Bible is God's authoritative revelation. And it tells us in no uncertain terms who God's people are.

This is the specific focus of the eleventh chapter of Romans. Verse 15, speaking of the Jews, says:

> **15 For if the casting away of them be the reconciling of the world, what shall the receiving of them be, but life from the dead?**

"Them" refers to Israel. "The world" is obviously everybody else. So this verse takes in the scope of history, and mentions how all the nations of the world fit into God's choice of a people. The rest of the chapter breaks the matter down into several easy steps, answering the question, "Who are God's people?"

Jews Were, and Some Still Are

The first part of the answer is that the Jews were the people of God, and some still are.

Chapter 10 ended on the sad note that Israel as a whole rejected Jesus as their Messiah. God held out his arms to them to welcome them into the kingdom, but they rejected the gospel that proclaimed their king to be Jesus Christ.

So Paul begins chapter 11 by asking, **Hath God cast away his people?** It seems a reasonable conclusion that he had. But it isn't the correct one. **God forbid,** says Paul. And he proves it: **I also am an Israelite** (v.1). If Israelites were now cast away, how could Paul—or any of the other first five thousand or more Christians—have been saved?

God hath not cast away his people which he foreknew (v.2). instead, the plan is more intricate, and involves God's intention to make sure that, even though Israel was often rebellious and idolatrous, he always had *some* Israelites who were faithful. Paul refers to the story of Elijah, who complained that "nobody" was faithful to God anymore, only he. But God told him, **I have reserved to myself seven thousand** (v.4). These, during Elijah's time, and others at other times, were what Paul then calls **a remnant according to the election of grace** (v.5). There have always been people who responded to the gracious call of God throughout history, who were counted righteous by their faith. This is the remnant. In times of revival in Israel, the remnant was more. In times of rebellion, it was far less. But there have always been some.

For Paul, then, he and the apostles, and the Jewish Christians of the first churches were the remnant. When offered their Messiah, they received him. But Paul reminds us, and himself, that even the remnant received Christ only because God gave them grace to do so: **If by grace, then it is no more of works** (v.6). **Israel** (v.7), meaning those of Israel the nation in general, have **not obtained that which he [they] seeketh.** Only **the election**, or the elect, the chosen, have obtained it—"it" being salvation. **The rest were blinded** (v.7).

To support this rather distressing statement about the Jews, Paul quotes David's Psalm 69, where he confesses God's sovereign right to hide the truth from some, while revealing it to others.

Anyone who reads this Psalm realizes that David probably saw a connection between his enemies' rebellious lives and God's blinding them. But in that Psalm he also admits to his own "foolishness" and "sins." Clearly he understood that God's choice of a people was not based on their merit, but on God's gracious and sovereign plan.

We can't know all the reasoning of God in his choice of the Jews. It is simply revealed as being part of his immense and perfect plan for this world. But there are some obvious practical reasons.

- Choosing one nation gave God a relatively cohesive group through which to tell a story and to reveal his principles for living and absolutes of righteousness.
- One nation became the family from whom a Savior could come, and that nation therefore represented the concept of the family of God.
- One people served as an example to the world of the continuous, gracious working of God.
- The choice of a people served as a focal point of God's plan, for the ultimate benefit of all humanity.

Walking outside just after sundown in early 2001, one could often glimpse for a minute or so the underbelly of the space station, as it skimmed across the sky more than 75 miles up. What a fantastic extreme from the first wood and cloth plane flown across the dunes by the Wright brothers nearly a hundred years before. Yet the Wrights, the Lindberghs, and others who pioneered flight, forged the way for the whole world to become routine air travelers. We hop aboard 747s with no thought of the danger and discovery of those first flights and the daring of those who made them. It's as if they were chosen to blaze the trail through the skies, and we were destined to follow, benefitting from their pilgrimage, their mistakes, their discipline, their faith, and their sacrifices.

Israel was something like that in history. Paul says in 1 Corinthians 10:11 that the experiences of the ancient Israelites were examples to us. Their history, how God worked among them, disciplined them, led them, blessed them, forgave them, taught them, were all meant to lead the way for many others to come.

Furthermore, Paul insists that Israel has not been **cast away** (v.1) or eliminated from the equation, just because God has broadened the scope of his calling. Paul hints at an exciting turn of events yet to come.

So the Jews were God's people, and some still are. Jewish Christians in our day are some of the more joyous and informed people of God on the earth. Who better to be followers of Messiah Jesus than Jews! But they are not the only people of God:

Gentiles Are, By Grace

The Gentiles also are the people of God, by grace.

God widened the scope of his chosen people to include Gentiles—everybody who isn't a Jew!—when the gospel first began to be preached. Any Gentile who believes on Jesus Christ becomes a son of Abraham by faith—like Isaac, the son by faith in God's promise.

Paul's Bible was the Old Testament, which clearly defines the Jews as the people of God's choice in history. Abraham was called out of Ur to be the father of a nation. Of Abraham's sons Ishmael and Isaac, Isaac was the son of promise. In Roman 9:7 Paul quotes Genesis 21:12: "In Isaac shall thy seed be called." The rest of the Old Testament is based on this historical choice of Isaacs' son and seed, Jacob, his twelve sons, and the tribes they begat.

When the Jews as a nation overwhelmingly refused to acknowledge Jesus as the Messiah, they **stumbled** (v.11). But they didn't do so **that they should fall** (v.11), but only so the Gentiles could flood into the kingdom as a result. Note the word *fall* here: our English in verse 11 says the Jews didn't stumble so they could *fall*, but so that through their *fall* salvation could come to Gentiles. It may sound confusing, but there are two words for *fall* in the Greek. One means "fall for good," and the other means "fall aside," or "take a misstep." It's the difference between falling off a cliff and just falling in the bushes beside the trail.

Israel fell beside the trail, and Gentiles entered the pathway from behind them and took the lead.

Israel's rejection of Christ was the open door to Gentile inclusion in the people of God—because God *will* have a people. In verses 17-24 Paul refers to Israel as the original olive tree, into which Gentiles, like wild olive branches, have been **grafted** (v.17). And he warns us Gentiles not to **boast** (v.18), because God can as easily turn history on its ear, harden Gentile hearts, and graft the **natural branches** (v.24) **into their own olive tree.**

In other words, he is putting tremendous stress on the grace of God that makes any of us part of the people of God at all.

A popular Christian broadcaster, the late J. Vernon McGee, used to begin his program by welcoming listeners aboard the "Bible bus." Salvation itself is something like a bus, taking travelers to the eternal kingdom of God. Where it stops is up to the driver, who is God, and how many it takes on is in his province, not ours.

It is vital for us to recognize that we are not in charge of the plan of salvation. It is God's plan. He draws whom he will to Christ, and how he does that in history is in his province. If we are included in his family, among his people, it is by his grace, not our own ingenuity or initiative. We must respond when he calls. But the calling is still his.

And that call will not extend endlessly. Just as Israel didn't have forever to be the exclusive people of God, even the Gentiles do not have all the time in the world. The basis of being part of the people of God has a sense of urgency to it, an urgency brought into even sharper focus by the third answer in Romans 11 to the question of who God's people are:

All Who Receive Christ Now

The people of God are all who receive Christ—*now.*

Paul says the offer of inclusion in the people of God is good only **until the fulness of the Gentiles be come in** (v.25). When that takes place, in some sense **all Israel shall be saved** (v.26), which along with other Bible passages suggests a great surge of Jews into the company of believers in Christ at the very end time. But as he uses the term "Israel" in v.26, Paul again means the children of Abraham by faith, all people who are born into the family of God by trusting in Christ.

Paul says this is God's fulfillment of the timeless nature of his covenant with the Jews, who are still **beloved for the fathers' sakes** (v.28), meaning the forefathers of the Jews who were given these promises. God's calling of the Jews, or of anyone, says Paul, is **without repentance** (v.29). He doesn't "take things back" once he has said them.

We have no idea how long this time of **mercy,** that Paul describes in verses 30-32, will last, but the implication is that time is marching swiftly toward its conclusion.

Even the idea of mercy in this chapter is pregnant with urgency. The opportunity for experiencing God's mercy is not held out to us forever. **God hath concluded them all in unbelief, that he might have mercy upon all,** Paul writes in v.32. It is reminiscent of Isaiah 55:6-7, which promise that "he will have mercy ...and abundantly pardon." That same offer, however, begins with these words: "Seek ye the Lord while he may be found; Call ye upon him while he is near."

Wise Christians did not make predictions of the return of Christ in the year 2000 or at the turn of the millennium—believers have been made fools by doing that in the past. Most recently, gullible people around the world were swept along with a tide of anticipation whipped up by Harold Camping, a California broadcaster, that the rapture would occur on May 21, 2011 and the world would end in cataclysm on October 21, 2011. Camping and his followers tucked their tails between their legs and slunk away when nothing happened. Many Christians, however, cannot shake the sense that we are closing rapidly on the day when the Lord will call a halt to this age and the end will come.

Books and movies like "Left Behind," which depicts one

scenario for the biblical period of tribulation and the second coming, have gained attention even in the secular world. The times are ripe to present to the world the urgent message of God's offer of mercy and inclusion in his saved people.

Who are the people of God? The Jews were—and some still are. The Gentiles became God's people by grace, when the Jews stumbled. In fact, anyone who comes to Christ in repentance and receives him by faith is included in the people of God.

It is no haphazard matter to God, however. Clearly he has not sat in heaven and said, "Come if you like, it doesn't matter to me." No, God has been working out a plan, ever since the beginning of time.

In fact, it is this sovereign plan that strikes the reader most about Romans 11. For this passage tells us that in observing the tides of human events, which in one respect are the cumulative result of the good and evil choices of men and nations, still one can see the hand of God, working out a plan, choosing and protecting a people. This is a wondrous paradox, that to us salvation comes about when we choose Christ, but to God it has always been about his choosing us. And it is a paradox that leads to the kind of doxology with which Paul closes the chapter.

He marvels at the **depth of the riches both of the wisdom and knowledge of God**, and at how **unsearchable** his **ways** are. Verse 34 tells us God had no **counsellor**, which means his wisdom is ultimate. He conceived this fantastic plan, and understands and controls everything to the nth degree—he doesn't need any help. **For of him, and through him, and to him, are all things.** When we understand this, truly begin to realize its significance, then we will say with Paul, **to [him] be glory for ever, Amen!** (v.36).

Many people are confused by the appearance of conflict between the ideas of man's free will and God's sovereign plan, between man's privilege of choosing, and God's right to choose. There really is no conflict—God understands it. That we don't is of little consequence.

The answer to the apparent conflict is that it is a miracle of

God. He has created a world in which we all may "choose whom we will serve" (cp. Joshua 24:15) without coercion. At the same time, he has mercy on whom he will, and whom he will he hardens (Romans 9:15). Both are true.

We needn't concern ourselves with figuring out God's part. Our focus should be on our own part, our response to the divine invitation to be members of God's family. And any of us may be, by exercising simple faith in Jesus Christ.

Christian Oughts

Romans 12

Some years ago a pastor proposed a new word for the English language: "oughtness." It's like responsibility or duty, but has a slightly different tone. The noun form would be simply "oughts." The definition is simple: An "ought" is something we ought to do. "Oughtness" is the need of something to be done.

Christians have some oughts in their lives. The Christian faith isn't simply a matter of signing on to *get* something, but of pledging to *be* something and to *do* something. True, salvation is what God does for us. But Christianity is not only salvation, but also discipleship. And discipleship has some oughts about it. The twelfth chapter of Romans is about some of these oughts.

The key verse of this chapter is 12:2:

> **2 And be not conformed to this world: but be ye transformed by the renewing of your mind, that ye may prove what is that good, and acceptable, and perfect, will of God.**

The oughtness of the Christian faith is based on one thing: the astounding, unfathomable, inestimably rich grace of God. Romans 11 ended a three-chapter discussion of God's tremendous grace. One cannot get a full grasp on its dimensions or significance. We are left simply to respond in the only appropriate way. That response is characterized by certain things—Christian oughts:

Consecration

The first of these *oughts* is consecration—being made holy unto God. When you read verse 2 you get the sense that the Christian should be wholly devoted to the purposes of God, instead of investing his life in the things that non-Christians do.

Verse one pictures the believer offering himself up to God much as the Old Testament worshiper would offer a sacrifice on the altar. Only we are not to be slain, but to live for Christ: **Present**

your bodies a living sacrifice, holy, acceptable unto God. Holy means set apart *from* sin and set apart *to* God. Christians are persons who are to be reserved for God's use.

We are **acceptable** as living sacrifices only because of the grace of God through the blood of Jesus Christ. Ephesians 1:6 says, "to the praise of the glory of his grace, wherein he hath made us accepted in the beloved." And because Christ has made this supreme sacrifice for us, our consecration is what Paul calls our **reasonable service.** These words may also be translated "spiritual worship." The heart of our worship as Christians is not superficial acts of symbolism, or memorized words spoken in ritual. It is the worship of committed lives, acting out of the depths of our spirits. It is focusing our whole beings on the goal of loving God and doing his will.

When we are consecrated this way, our lives will be a proving ground for the perfect will of God, demonstrating how his will is the best and most fulfilling plan for us (v.2).

In March of 1991 the *Charlotte Observer* carried an article about Henry Pulsifer, who walked into Lincolnton, N.C. carrying a cross. Pulsifer's story was that he was dying from a cancerous tumor in his chest when he became convinced God wanted him to preach the gospel from Kiln, Mississippi to the Canadian wilderness. Immediately he constructed a cross, put wheels on its end, and began walking. He walked all the way to Canada, and along the way, he says the cancer disappeared. He never stopped walking. He and his wife, Ann, walked Americas highways, carrying the cross and taking the opportunity to preach the gospel wherever people would listen.

There is no way to predict how God will bless you when your life becomes completely consecrated to him. Many things you can choose to do in this world are both enjoyable and good. However, the Christian has a mandate to devote himself to the things of God and to discover and be engaged in doing God's will. Only in doing his **good, acceptable and perfect** will (v.2) are we perfectly fulfilled.

Service

Since consecration to God means being devoted to his will, it suggests the second Christian *ought:* service. Our lives should be characterized by humble service to and for the Lord.

The Bible's definition of the Christian's humility is both simple and unparalleled: **not to think of himself more highly than he ought to think** (v.3). We ought to realize our worth as human beings, and our preciousness to God, but we ought not to think of ourselves as inherently better than others, as lords of the church, as people who should be served. We ought to think of ourselves as servants of others.

Paul says we're like the **members** (or parts) **of one body,** and that we're **one** in Christ (v.5). Consequently we have **gifts differing according to the grace that is given to us** (v.6). We are to use these gifts, like **prophecy** (v.6), **ministry, teaching** (v.7), **exhortation,** the ability to govern or lead, or a special heart of **mercy** (v.8), to serve one another, as Jesus would do.

It's interesting that these descriptions of service mention **ministry** (v.7)—which frequently involves unseen acts of helping—and ruling (v.8), which is taking charge of an organization, a decidedly public role. These are essentially opposite one another, yet both can constitute service. This demonstrates that service is not so much what is done, but the spirit and motivation in which it is done, and the benefit it renders to the kingdom of God as a result.

Anyone who has had bad "service" in a restaurant knows this difference first hand. Sometimes you wouldn't describe what took place as service at all.

Service is defined by humility, a spirit of willingness to be of help to someone else, a selfless attitude, with no personal, hidden agenda, and no extra baggage of resentment.

An unknown someone wrote a little verse called "Sharing" that is really about service:

If you have a gift, bring it.
If you have a song, sing it.
If you have a talent, use it.
If you have love, diffuse it.
If you have sadness, bear it.
If you have gladness, share it.
If you have happiness, give it.
If you have salvation, live it.
If you have a prayer, pray it.
If you have a kind word, say it.
We all have gifts that we may bring.
We all have songs that we may sing.
We all have kind words we may say.
We all have prayers that we may pray.
We all have love and joy to give,
And what a joy life is to live,
If we just scatter everywhere
These things God's given us to share.[2]

Character

If the first two *oughts* of the Christian, consecration and service, are pictured as sides of a triangle, then the base of that triangle is character, the third *ought.* Service without character is legalism. Consecration without character is not consecration, but hypocrisy.

Fully half of Romans 12 is a litany of character traits that ought to describe every believer: genuine **love**, and purity of life (v.9) lead the list, followed by affectionate kindness and deference (v.10), industriousness and dedication (v.11), joy and patience (v.12), generosity (v.13), empathy (v.15), and a complete lack of a vengeful spirit (vv.14-19)—in other words, a forgiving heart. And, we are told to **condescend to men of low estate** (v.16).

It's interesting how some words have attained the opposite of

---

[2] Source unknown at present

their original meaning. In the English Bible, reflecting hundreds of years of usage, to condescend meant to get down on someone's level and adapt to his needs so as to help and communicate. Now, more often than not, to condescend means to treat someone with an air of superiority. It has attained this meaning because of the tendency of some to act *as if* they were coming down to another level to help, while in actuality they were exaggerating their efforts to showcase their superiority.

This may be just the point of this passage: our love is to be **without dissimulation** (v.9). We are genuinely to **be of the same mind one toward another** (v.16), not just as a show. Our character is to be righteous, not self-righteous, holy, not merely holier-than-thou.

Christian character doesn't come naturally, as if being a Christian for forty years automatically results in holiness rubbing off on us. Character has to be built, worked at, practiced. The last verse of Romans 12 soberly advises us, **Be not overcome of evil, but overcome evil with good** (v.21). Unless we resist temptation, resist the direction the world flows in, and steer against the tide, our character will look like the unbelieving world, not like a follower of Christ. People, like rivers, become crooked by following the path of least resistance.

A man was campaigning in a rural race for a senate seat. One rainy night a man knocked at his door and said, "I need help. My car is stalled down the road."

The candidate slogged through rain and mud, arriving soaked, ready to do whatever necessary. When the owner got in and turned the key, the car started fine. "Looks like nothing's wrong," said the would-be senator.

"I know," said the man. "I also know this state needs a good man in Washington. I wanted to know if you were that kind of man. Now I do."[3]

---

[3]Joe Trull, in *Proclaim*, The Sunday School Board of the Southern Baptist Convention, (Nashville, TN, J-A-S, 1987) 30.

Would you pass the character test?

Character is not just for politicians and businessmen. In fact, if a Christian teen does not build godly character while young, he or she may dig a spiritual rut never to be gotten out of.

Somebody dubbed the following list of Christian oughts as "The Teen Commandments"—author unknown:

1. Don't let your parents down: they brought you up.
2. Choose your companions with care: you become what they are.
3. Master your habits or they will master you.
4. Treasure your time: don't spend it, invest it.
5. Stand for something or you'll fall for anything.
6. Date only someone who would make a good mate.
7. See what you can do for others, not what they can do for you.
8. Guard your thoughts: what you think, you are.
9. Don't fill up on this world's crumbs: feed your soul on Living Bread.
10. Give your all to Christ: he gave his all for you.[4]

Good advice for character building, wouldn't you say?

There is a certain interconnectedness about these three Christian *oughts:* consecration, service, character. We owe consecration to God. We owe service to both God and one another. And we owe character to God, each other, and ourselves. In order to keep from being cardboard cutouts of Christianity, we really *ought* to be consecrated servants of the highest character.

One of the oldest defenses against the gospel is that becoming a Christian will "spoil all my fun." There's a major element of falsehood in that, because Christians have fun, too, and living a truly holy life for the Lord is joyful. But there's an element of truth

---

[4] Author Unknown, published in Pulpit Helps, ed. Spiros Zodhiates, Jan 1993 (Chattanooga, TN, AMG Publishers), 13.

in it, too. If someone insists on defining fun as worldliness, and is committed to pursuing worldly habits, vices and goals as his highest enjoyment in life, then becoming a Christian will, indeed, spoil his fun. The true Christian will adopt a sense of *oughtness* about his life. He will be consecrated to God and will seek God's will for his life. He will live not only for himself, but also to serve and help others. And he will shuck the rough and seedy character of worldliness and bear the fruit of the Spirit instead.

The pressure to relax, go with the flow and just conform to the world is tremendous, and it's certainly easier as a way of life. But when we think, really think deeply, about the magnificence of the grace of God toward us in Jesus Christ, who not only came to us, but also lived for us, died for us and rose again, aren't there some things we really *ought* to do to say "thanks?"

How Much Do We Owe?

Romans 13

All of us have heard, and some of us have said, "I owe you a debt of gratitude." What does that mean?—that someone says, "Thank you," and then goes off never to think of the matter again? Hardly. To owe a debt of gratitude is to feel appreciation so deeply and profoundly that you live continually with the realization of how good someone has been to you.

Consider the works of God as they have been described in the first 12 chapters of Romans: how God was merciful to us in our sins, how he sent Jesus Christ to die in our place, how Christ rose from the grave so we could be raised to new life, and how we are free of condemnation and have great power in the Holy Spirit. If you have received Christ as Savior, you are the beneficiary of all this! Now, consider your debt of gratitude.

We who know Christ personally owe God an unpayable debt. This hardly means we should neglect our obligation to thank God, however. On the contrary, we are obliged to do whatever we can to show our love and thanks to him. We ought to ask each day, *how much do we owe?*

The thirteenth chapter of Romans answers this question for us. The heart of the chapter is verse 8:

> **8   Owe no man any thing, but to love one another: for he that loveth another hath fulfilled the law.**

This verse calls to mind Jesus' answer to someone who asked him what the greatest commandment was. His answer was, "Love the Lord thy God." And the second, he said, was to "love thy neighbor as thyself."

The New Testament letter of James (who was Jesus brother, by the way) speaks of loving our neighbors as the "royal law" (Jas.2:8).

So when we read in Romans 13:8 that love fulfills the law, it reminds us that whatever we owe God or man is summed up in our living out this all-encompassing love, from the bottom of our hearts.

That might be the simplest answer to what we owe, but Romans 13 fills in the major areas of how this love is to be expressed. In what is clearly the reverse order of their importance, here are the things we owe God for what he has done for us:

Good People in the World

First is to be good people in the world. In specific, Paul focuses on our duties to be good, law abiding citizens.

Obviously, when we say of someone that he or she is a really good person, we often mean much more than that he or she obeys the law. We may be talking about qualities of love, compassion, personal integrity, and so on. Certainly we should be good people in these ways, but Paul's emphasis at the top of this chapter is on the public image of Christians in the Roman Empire. He is thinking about the way Christians are perceived by those in authority, because the reputation of Christians and Christianity in general will have much to do with how well the road is paved for the gospel to penetrate society.

Paul teaches us we are to **be subject unto the higher powers** (v.1). He means the duly authorized government of a people.

To be subject means to obey the law of the land. Why are we to express this kind of citizenship? Because there is **no power but of God.** Governments are **ordained of God** (v.1). Paul means that God wills that sinful man be under governmental authority, so that order can be kept and wrongdoers can be punished. **Rulers,** says Paul, are **a terror** to **the evil [works]** (v.3). Governments bear **the sword** (v.4), which means they are authorized to punish wrongdoing. A ruler, or a government, therefore, is **the minister of God to thee for good** (v.4).

Because government is part of God's plan, Paul says, **whosoever therefore resisteth the power, resisteth the ordinance of God** (v.2).

Paul's main concern in this chapter was to warn Christians against anarchy, the idea that because we know God and his law, we can ignore the laws of our governments, on the premise that we are now above them.

So Paul says there are two reasons we should be good, law abiding citizens: **for wrath** (v.5), meaning we will be deservingly punished if we don't, and **for conscience sake** (v.5), meaning it's what God requires of us. In other words, we should obey the law not just so we won't be caught, but because it's the right thing to do.

It's not very hard to obey the law in countries where government is based on principles derived from the Bible. It may be difficult, however, in places where laws are oppressive, or where they restrict religious belief, deny freedom, or require immoral actions. In fact, this teaching of God's word has provoked many an hour of reflection and debate among Christians. Many people can't understand how a believer in Jesus Christ could always obey every law in a land where Christ is hated or rulers seek to destroy Christianity.

Perhaps what makes this passage controversial is the assumption that Paul means we must always obey *every* law, under *every* government, regardless. Certainly he doesn't list exceptions when telling us to submit to government. But just as certain is that he would not disagree with Peter and the other apostles, who under orders to keep quiet about Jesus Christ, said, "We ought to obey God rather than men" (Acts 5:29). Earlier, they had responded to similar edicts by saying, "We cannot but speak the things which we have seen and heard" (Acts 4:20). Indeed, the whole history of the early church—including Paul's life—is filled with examples of Christians insisting on carrying out the great commission *in defiance of orders from the government.*

So what is the answer to the apparent conflict of instructions in the Bible? Viewing the Bible as a whole, perhaps we can best express the answer in this principle: Where government does not require us to disobey God or keep us from obeying God, obey it. Where government demands that we disobey God, we must obey him first, and accept the consequences.

In a book written in the mid 1960s, the Christian author, commenting on this very passage, said, "Never should a Christian resort to civil disobedience."[5] That statement is indefensible biblically. Further, in the light of the righteous goal of the Civil Rights Movement of the 50s and 60s, it is difficult to see how a Christian could say it is never, ever, permissible for a Christian to disobey unjust laws in order to change them—if no other remedy is available.

And there's where the stress is. Paul is forceful in what he says about obeying governments because God wants us to exhaust all legal avenues to pursue his will in the world, because disorder and unrest do not help the cause of Christ. They threaten it.

Again, why must we be good citizens? Because we owe God a debt of love, and love means being a blessing to the world for the sake of the gospel, that it might flourish in peace.

Love to Fellow Man

Our obligation to government is one of those grand, sweeping duties that seem bigger than our everyday lives, sometimes. But it's really just an extension of a more local and immediate duty—the *master obligation* of the Christian: to love our fellow man.

The Christian's Master Obligation is master in the same sense as a master key. It fits all the doors in a certain building. There are individual locks, and individual keys that fit each one, and none of them fits the others, but the master key fits them all.

The master obligation of the Christian, love for all persons, fits all circumstances. The details are different for one person to another, and no two relationships are alike, but love is the key to building every relationship, the key to every heart, the key to every solution to every problem, the key to knowing what to do in any circumstance.

God's word says in verse 8 of this chapter to **owe no man any thing, but to love one another.** Some say this means we should

---

[5] John Phillips, *Exploring Romans* (Chicago, Moody Press, 1969), 218.

never incur financial debt. That interpretation really does not fit the context. This command to **owe no man** means we are not to leave any debt *outstanding* or to be enslaved by any obligation. No one should have us over a barrel. If anyone does, his command over us may keep us from living in the will of God.

The only obligation that we should have toward others that we know we will never fully repay is the obligation of love, love for them because of our love of God.

Doing one good deed for someone doesn't pay our debt in full. If another circumstance arises where our action is called for, what must we do? We still must love. We owe love without end.

Paul illustrates his meaning himself, saying in verse 9 that laws against **adultery, stealing, false witness,** and **covet**ing, as well as any other commandment, are just applications of the master rule of love. If we love, we won't steal, or lie, and so on. Because love **worketh no ill to his neighbour** (v.10).

A brief study of the Bible's various statements concerning how we are to treat *one another* illustrates what this master obligation of love is all about.

We are to be devoted to one another and outdo one another in showing honor (Rom.12:10). We are to rejoice with one another (Rom.12:15), and weep with one another (Rom.12:15). We are not to judge one another (Rom.14:13) but to receive one another (Rom.15:17). We are to greet one another (Rom.16:16) and counsel one another (Rom.15:14). These statements are all from this one letter to the Romans!

That's not all. We are to serve one another, be kind to one another, forgive one another, be tenderhearted toward and encourage one another. We are to submit to one another, forbear and minister to one another, not to speak evil against one another, not to grumble against one another, but to confess our faults to one another, and pray for one another. And we are to fellowship with one another and bear one another's burdens. And the list goes on.

But all these "one anothers" are summed up in the master

obligation to one another: "Love one another" (John 13:34-35). Jesus gave us that command, called it a new commandment, and said that if we obeyed it, it would identify us as the people of God, his disciples. It's the one thing that sums up what we owe to everyone we meet.

Putting that commandment into action is the challenge, isn't it? Because some people aren't very loveable. Sometimes, neither are we. That's why we need to forgive one another, so we can go on loving one another, and so fulfill the law of Christ.

Our debt of gratitude to God obliges me to love you because God loves you. And it obliges you to love me because God loves me. But our debt of gratitude means we have one obligation greater than all others:

Holiness and All to God

We owe God holy living and everything we are and have. All we have will never pay the debt, but nothing less than all is appropriate as a payment.

There is a sense of urgency about our responding to God in this surrender, since **the night is far spent,** and **the day is at hand** (v.12). Paul says we need to **awake out of sleep,** and he speaks of the **nearness** of **our salvation.** He's talking about the return of Christ. If it was true then, it's 2,000 years truer now!

What does he say we must do? **Cast off the works of darkness... put on the armour of light** (v.12). Be **honest,** don't party and get drunk (v.13), and stop being envious and contentious with each other (striving, v.13). Put in positive terms, we are to **put on the Lord Jesus Christ** (v.14). Let him clothe us with his righteousness before God and with his righteous life and power before all men. We are also to **make not provision for the flesh** (v.14), which means we are to deny our sinful impulses any opportunity to be fulfilled—not even to toy with the idea.

A little boy was told by his mother not to eat any of the freshly baked cookies she had just put in the cookie jar on the shelf. A half hour later she returned to the kitchen to find him seated at the table, the cookie jar open in front of him, a lone cookie on a napkin beside it, and him with his hands in his lap. She said, "I told you not to eat a cookie!"

He answered innocently, "I'm not, Mom. I'm just looking at it!"

That's making **provision for the flesh**, and it is just a short step away from **fulfill**ing **the lusts thereof** (v.14). To be holy unto God, we must put away temptation, and not toy with sin.

In 2 Kings 23, we learn of king Josiah's reign. He followed Manasseh and Amon, two exceedingly wicked kings. Josiah went about setting things right. And the chapter is verse upon verse about how he broke down altars, burned vessels, tore down sodomite's havens, and crushed idols to powder. It goes on and on, until Josiah is finished, and the kingdom of the Israelites holds the Passover feast, celebrating God's saving grace, and committing their lives to him who delivered them.

That's what we owe God! Holiness, and our all. Leave nothing standing in our lives that opposes him! Give all we are and have to serve him!

How much do we owe? Being good people in society is the least of it. Loving one another genuinely is more important. Loving God with the consecration of our lives is our greatest debt. We can never retire that debt. But we should go from here to glory gladly paying on it.

Solving Our Differences
Romans 14

It would be wonderful if we could become Christians and instantly be just like Christ. The church would be a perfect place to enjoy life, where God's voice would be heard clearly in our fellowship, nothing would ever go wrong, all of us would know the will of God, and we would experience ideal faith, commitment and involvement.

But it has never happened, and it never will, as long as we are in this world. We are born into the kingdom of God as baby believers, and we must grow into Christlikeness. Not only are there differing levels of spiritual growth as we develop, but even believers who are nearly the same place in their spiritual maturity sometimes have differences of belief, often about relatively minor things.

How do we solve our differences? Do we follow the democratic model and put them to a vote? Do we look to an autocratic model, where one person's view is law? Do we ignore differences and hope they'll go away?

Romans 14 gives us some principles for solving our differences. Paul has guided his readers through the basics of our need of salvation and God's provision of a Savior. And having talked a little about the kind of lives we owe God, now he gives us some very practical guidance on how to solve the differences that tug and stretch the fabric of our fellowship. His goal is that we might live united before the world, showing the world's people how God's people behave.

The core verse of this chapter is verse 20, and in particular, the first part of it, which says:

20 For meat destroy not the work of God.

That statement dramatically summarizes the overarching principle: Don't hurt the church over things that are not central to the Christian faith. Stated positively it would be this: What unifies us and gives us our purpose are the great and central truths of God's word and our salvation. We should join hands around these things, and handle all other issues with grace, love, and deference.

What brought up this discussion in the first place was an issue about food. Paul uses the particular to discuss the general, and gives us some wonderful principles for solving our differences.

Each Believer Can Know God for Himself

The first of these principles is that each believer can know God for himself. God has given us his inspired, inerrant word, and each believer can read and understand it for himself without the necessity of any priest to interpret it for him. God still calls preachers and teachers in his church; as they themselves learn and grow, their function is to pass on their insights to the rest of us, which helps us. In reality, however, any of us can help any other person as we all grow and learn together. Every believer can know God and understand God's truth and God's will from the Bible and in his own experience, for himself. It requires study and learning, but no special anointing or ordination to understand the word of God or know the Lord.

This principle means that when we have disagreements, we need to understand that people have a right to reach conclusions on their own about matters. Not all conclusions are right, and many people form terribly uninformed opinions. Nevertheless, in trying to solve differences of opinion, no one of us can claim inherently to have a straighter line to God than another.

What brought this up in Rome was a matter of eating meat. Paul had discussed with the Corinthians the matter of eating meat offered to idols, but the situation in Rome appears to have been the broader issue of vegetarianism.

Verse 2 says that some eat **all things** and others, whom Paul describes as **weak,** eat only **herbs**—vegetables. It wasn't just that some did and some didn't, but that they argued about it, as if it were crucial to their fellowship, or as if neither side could rest until they had put the other side in its place.

Paul's instructions for solving this dispute put the burden on those who ate meat, saying they were to **receive him that is weak in the faith** (v.1), i.e. those who were vegetarians for religious reasons. So he weighs in on the dispute right away, but quickly says this doesn't make it right *to force agreement as a condition of fellowship.* (This is the meaning of **doubtful disputations** in v.1). So we're not to settle differences by insisting that we agree first. *Not in matters that are not central to our faith.*

Christians have always recognized these verses to be about debatable issues, not crucial Christian doctrine. No one is going to fail to be saved or fail to grow in Christ because he is a vegetarian, even if he arrives at his opinion on faulty biblical analysis. Being or not being a meat eater isn't going to affect your Christianity very much.

There are other issues that are minor by comparison. They vary from place to place and time to time. What God's word says very forcefully is that we are to solve these issues first by recognizing that they are *not* crucial, and then by agreeing that we have a right to reach conclusions for ourselves, because we're all on level ground when it comes to knowing God and his truth.

Paul points to this equality by saying that if you look beyond the dispute, each party is acting **unto the Lord.** And each party **giveth God thanks.** In their minds, they are devoting their conduct to God. And since the conduct itself is not a matter of morals or ethics, but morally neutral activities, there is a sense in which it doesn't matter which side they're on. What is important is that we live **unto the Lord** and **die unto the Lord,** but in any event **we are the Lord's** (v.8). And we need not only to proclaim this about ourselves, but also to admit and proclaim it about others, even if we disagree with them about some things.

Sometimes this is the only way to solve differences: to agree to disagree, and to reassert our unity with others in our faith in Christ.

Every Believer is Accountable to God for Himself

If each believer can know God and his word for himself, then it follows that every believer is accountable to God for himself. This is the second principle for solving our differences.

Why dost thou judge thy brother? Paul asks in v.10. And he gives the sense of the word "judge" in his next phrase—and it's good that he did, because there's so much confusion about what judging means. He says, **Or why dost thou set at nought thy brother?** Why do you make him "nothing," belittle him or regard him as worthless, and all on the basis of things that aren't even central to the faith!

The problem is, the Roman Christians were inclined—and aren't we all—to measure one another by themselves and evaluate their own worth by the diminished worth of others. There was a stern reminder in Paul's words that **every knee shall bow... and every tongue shall confess to God** (v.11). If we become too confident about how right we are in relations with others, we will face an embarrassing situation or worse when we all face the judge of all of us, and the truth is known.

A little girl announced at breakfast one morning that she had grown; she was now six feet tall. Her parents were mystified by the announcement. They had been measuring her periodically for growth and development. But she had taken the job on for herself that day, and not being able to find the ruler, she took out a piece of paper and made one for herself. Sure enough, she measured six feet tall, by her ruler.

Elsewhere in the scripture Paul says "they measuring themselves by themselves and comparing themselves among themselves are not wise (2 Cor.10:12). The only one certified to judge with 100% accuracy is God, because he is the only Holy One, and his is the only perfect yardstick.

Rather than putting other people down for the things they don't agree with us about, we should be concentrating instead on not putting any **stumblingblock or an occasion to fall** (v.13) in their way. This means we must avoid what we call doing things "in your face." If we defy other's qualms or convictions, what may happen is that they may adopt our beliefs or practices, but against their consciences. In other words, only half convinced, they go along because they fear being ridiculed if they don't.

Some people would regard this as simply having won the dispute. But what really happens is that people damage their own ability to hold true to their principles. And if they cave in over the non-essentials, they may cave in when it comes to truly important things. In either case, it's sin for them to undermine their own strength of will.

Paul takes the case of eating meat, and explains it. He does two things:

First he takes a position on it. It may be officially a debatable issue, but it isn't without a final solution. In this case, it's the vegetarians who don't have an adequate understanding of scripture: **there is nothing unclean of itself** (v.14). There's nothing wrong about eating meat. You may choose to be a vegetarian or vegan for your own estimation of the health benefits, but the overall view of the Bible does not support the conclusion that a Christian must not eat meat.

After weighing in on the specific matter, however, Paul points out what those who are stronger in faith and understanding may be disregarding unfairly: **but to him that esteemeth any thing to be unclean, to him it is unclean** (v.14). This makes all the difference in the world. There may not be anything wrong with something, but if you think there is, and you do it, you are sinning. Because as verse 20 says, **it is evil for that man who eateth with offence.**

And why would anyone do what he thinks is wrong? Actually, we all do it frequently. Sometimes we just succumb to temptation. However, people will also do things they think are wrong because of pressure, cajoling, ridicule, or the implied threat of belittlement, if they don't. This is why Paul says **if thy brother be grieved with thy meat, now walkest thou not charitably.** Intimidating others into behavior they are not comfortable with does not demonstrate Christian love.

And so often, these disagreements over one behavior or another have little to do with what Christian faith is all about. As Paul concludes, **For the kingdom of God is not meat and drink, but righteousness, and peace, and joy in the Holy Ghost** (v.17). Or as we could restate it from verse 20, "Don't wreck the fellowship over food."

Somebody said there are two good rules in life: (1) Don't sweat the small stuff; and (2) It's all small stuff. Well, it isn't *all* small stuff, but a lot of it is, and we tend to magnify the importance of things and demand that people agree with us on most or all of it. This is what aggravates disagreements. Sometimes, we simply have to agree to disagree.

All Believers Must Live for More than Themselves

Since each believer can know God's will and truth *for* himself, he can arrive at what he believes *by* himself. But since each of us has the same privilege, each is responsible to God for his own beliefs and actions. That can mean only one thing for solving our differences: we must live not just for ourselves and what we believe, but with great thoughtfulness toward others in what they believe.

To put it another way, conviction about our own living, and deference to the sincere differences of others, are two keys to peace in the fellowship of the church.

In the final three verses of chapter 14 Paul says three things:

*   Live out your convictions humbly before God. In v.22 he directs those who have **faith** about one of these debatable things to have it **to thyself before God**. The Greek "to" means "toward." Paul means we aren't to be obsessed with changing other people's minds about these less-than-essential things. Once the difference is recognized, we must not go overboard to make an issue of it. R.C.H. Lenski says, "The trouble is that we see the other man's faults and constantly want to doctor him whereas we ourselves still make a good patient."

- Respect those who have different convictions. In v.21 Paul says **it is good** not to do anything **whereby thy brother stumbleth.** In other words, we are at our best when we don't flaunt our conduct such that others are plunged into doubt about theirs or simply become upset and argumentative unnecessarily. We can't avoid people's taking offense at some things, but we can avoid using our own actions to provoke controversy without righteous reason.
- Finally, learn this important rule: **whatsoever is not of faith is sin** (v.23). If you aren't confident it's okay, it isn't, whether it is or not. Get it? And if you are confident on good, biblical grounds, rejoice in the Lord as you do good.

Christians will always have differences on some things. Coming from different backgrounds and assumptions, we will see things in different ways. Some differences will define religions altogether. Some will define denominations. Others are far less important and need not define anything at all except what we prefer. The key to Christian living is to know what is crucial and what isn't, and to love and work with each other in spite of disagreements on things that aren't matters of earthshaking importance.

In other words, solving our differences is usually a matter of exalting our agreement, and letting the rest dissolve in the gracious shadow of Christian love.

Mission: Imperative
Romans 15

In the TV series and more recently in the movies by the same name, *Mission Impossible,* a team called—appropriately—the "Impossible Mission Force" is given a mission that is dangerous, adventuresome, and downright near to impossible. That's why at the end of the recorded message giving the assignment the deep voice says, "Your mission, should you accept it, is to…" Then it's up to the team to accept or reject the mission.

Did you ever notice, if you followed the TV show, the team never turned a mission down? Can you imagine it—"Look, Jim, we could all be blown to bits. I vote no." "That's true, Jim, too hard. Nope, no go." Of course, there would be no TV show, either.

But the other reason, within the framework of the story itself, is that if the Mission Impossible team didn't accept these missions, they wouldn't exist as a team much longer. Whoever funded them would say, "I'll get me some guys who *will!"*

Out on a hillside near Jerusalem, Jesus prepares to disappear into heaven. He says to his disciples, "The harvest is plenteous, but the laborers are few. Your mission, should you decide to accept it, is to tell the gospel to the world." Is that what it says?

To the contrary, it says, "All power (authority) is given to me in heaven and earth. Go ye therefore and make disciples of all nations." There is no hint that this is an option. Since Jesus has the power, and Jesus is in us, it's not "mission impossible." Since Jesus commanded us, clearly it's mission imperative.

The fifteenth chapter of Romans covers a lot of territory, but at its heart it's about this mission imperative. The key verses in this chapter are 20-21:

20 Yea, so have I strived to preach the gospel, not where Christ was named, lest I should build upon another man's foundation:

21 But as it is written, To whom he was not spoken of,

they shall see: and they that have not heard shall understand.

These verses describe how the message of salvation in Christ comes to people who have never heard it, and produces repentance and saving faith, and they are converted. Much of this chapter is Paul's description of his own sense of calling to preach the gospel. But we must not miss his message. As he describes his own calling to the Roman Christians, he is really urging upon them the mission imperative of the church: to share Jesus Christ with its world.

Touching Neighbors With Hope

Just as Jesus began his description of the scope of the disciples' mission with Jerusalem—their immediate environment—so Paul approaches the subject of the church's mission at the local level. The church is to touch its neighbors with hope.

Where is that in chapter fifteen? Well, the chapter begins by summing up the discussion in chapter fourteen about keeping differences between Christians from destroying their unity. Paul says the **strong ought to bear the infirmities of the weak** (v.1), like Christ, who **pleased not himself** (v.2). Then he quotes Psalm 69:9, a messianic passage that talks prophetically about how Christ would bear the **reproaches** (v.3) of others. He did so in order to accomplish the plan of redemption and then reach the unsaved with his love. And Paul says this was written **for our learning** (v.4). As we become peacemakers like Christ, we will, through **patience and consolation** become **likeminded toward one another** (v.5), so that **with one mind and one mouth** we may **glorify God, even the Father of our Lord Jesus Christ** (v.6).

Clearly Paul is not talking about unity for the sake of mere happiness. He's talking about unity as a means to witness: the unified voice of the church glorifying God in the world around it.

And this is vital for us to understand, because it is a church's lack of unity that erects one of the greater barriers to a

community's acceptance of the gospel. The church's neighbors
need to see and hear the unanimous message of the church's
members that Jesus Christ is God's Son (v.6). This is what gives
people hope, light, and the promise of life eternal.

Jesus is our best example of touching neighbors with hope.
Paul says Jesus was the **minister of the circumcision** (v.8), a
reference to the fact that Jesus came to Israel *first.* Then he says
that Jesus also came **that the *Gentiles* might glorify God for his
mercy,** (v.9), which means obviously that Gentiles first must be
saved and then thank God for their salvation. He refers to Psalm
18:49, Deuteronomy 32:43, and Psalm 117:1, all of which mention
"Gentiles" (or "nations"). The point is that the gospel of Christ
came first to Jews, then to Gentiles, and since that's everyone, the
gospel is directed at all humanity.

Some of the Roman readers were Jews, some Gentiles, and
their neighbors were obviously the same, probably mostly Gentiles.
The message could not be clearer: the Roman Christians were to
touch their neighbors with the gospel of hope—the gospel that
causes the Gentiles to **glorify God** and **sing unto thy name,** and
laud him (vv.9-11).

Sometimes, Christians who have been in church all their lives
aren't in touch with what is going on in the secular mind. Many
non-Christians not only don't *have* eternal hope, but also
frequently *realize* they don't have it, and they live in such a way as
to distract themselves from their spiritual condition. In fact, that
explains much "worldly" behavior.

A few years ago Lee Strobel wrote a book called "Inside the
Mind of Unchurched Harry & Mary." It was intended to educate
longtime Christians to the spiritual emptiness of the non-
Christian, and to convince the church that the gospel *is* needed,
and *will* be received by some, because they know they need it.

Reaching Nations with Christ

Touching our neighbors with hope is vital to an individual
church's growth. But we cannot stop with what enlarges the

individual congregation. The mission imperative of the church is also reaching nations with Christ.

Paul says he has written much of what he has to remind the Romans of what he calls **the grace that is given to me of God, that I should be the minister of Jesus Christ to the Gentiles, ministering the gospel of God** (vv.15-16). He is a missionary to the nations abroad. Especially is he a missionary to new places—**I have strived to preach the gospel, not where Christ was named…but… to whom he was not spoken of** (vv.20-21). And he says in v.22, "**For which cause also I have been much hindered from coming to you.**" 'Sorry I haven't been to visit recently, but I was too busy preaching the gospel all over the world!'

That would be a good excuse for just about anything. The church's mission imperative is to reach nations with Christ.

It's irrelevant that you, personally, may not have been called to be a missionary to far off nations. You have a role to play that enables you to fulfill this mission imperative. First, you must be a good steward, by giving proportionately of your income, to underwrite the ministry of the church. Second, you should make certain your church gives to mission causes beyond itself. And third, if you're still young, you might reevaluate whether or not you might, in fact, be called to missions. No doubt many men and women God has led to be directly involved in missions have never known it, because they were too intent on their own career goals or too distracted by worldly things.

Paul was going to Jerusalem to take benevolence to the poor church there. But right afterwards, it was off to **Spain** (v.24), and he was blunt in saying to the Roman church, "**I trust to see you in my journey, and to be brought on my way thitherward by you** (v.24). That's his usual way of saying he hopes they will contribute to his mission work with money and material needs.

Supporting the Mission with Prayer

Touching our neighbors with hope and reaching the nations with Christ require that a church—let's make that personal—require that individual Christians come to terms with the mission imperative Jesus gave us on the Mount of Olives and in the upper room and really throughout his ministry. But this mission imperative also involves something else vital to its success from start to finish: we must support the mission with prayer.

Paul urged the Romans to pray for him. He uses that word **beseech** in verse 30 when asking them to **strive together** in prayer for him. And he gives them specifics—specific needs and specific prayer is always best. He asks them to pray about the situation in Judea where many **do not believe** and have persecuted him and all Christians there. And he asks them to pray **that I may come unto you with joy by the will of God** (v.32). He hopes to be successful and then have a time of rest and refreshing when he was able to visit them.

One of the greatest things missionaries impress upon us from the mission fields is the importance of praying for them. Many of us know, because we know our own weaknesses, that most of us don't take that need anywhere near seriously enough. Most of us, if the truth be told, are not aware of the reality of the spiritual battle being waged all around us, especially on mission fields where the gospel is rarely heard and the kingdom of the prince of darkness is strong.

Prayer is the link between those who go, those who enable them to go, and the one who sends us out to evangelize. Somehow God has made us responsible for praying for missions. He has put us in the equation. We may not understand how it works, but we must believe that it *does* work, and we must *do it*.

A college professor signed up to receive daily email with prayer needs for missionaries. Some were general—praying for a missionary by name on his birthday. Others were specific—a real need from a particular field, like a challenge to reach a hostile group, or courage to stand before staunch resistance. The number of requests was more than he could pray for. But he said it convinced him the need is great, and urgent.

The typical church may not be able to simply launch into

prayer for missions. The typical church is mired in many superficial and insignificant things. The typical church is not spiritually mature enough to sense the importance of much prayer, or to stay interested long in things that by their nature demand surrender, and real commitment.

Jesus called us to be different, not typical. He gave us an imperative that demands we achieve the extraordinary. Paul tells the Romans, and us: There's a world out there that needs the gospel. It starts in your own neighborhood, and goes around the globe. Touch those around you with Christ. Reach those beyond you by giving. Help send those God commissions. Pray for all who go and tell. Develop a sense of vision for the need of the lost world. It's your Mission: Imperative!

The People Who Make It Work
Romans 16

Advertisers for local businesses and institutions often use a kind of promotion that instead of focusing on products or services, puts the spotlight on people. A bank will advertise, "We're friends you can trust." A grocery store may say, "Our people make the difference." In some cases, that couldn't be more true. Two stores may be comparable in every way but one, the quality of people who work there. Where you find people who make it pleasant to do business, it really is the people who make the difference.

It's nowhere truer than with a church. We have heard many times that the church is not a building; it's people. There would be no church if there were no people. There is no product, no drive-through, automated service. There is nothing but the people, what they do together, and what they do for one another and for others. There is a message, and there is a Lord; but without the people the message evaporates and the Lord works elsewhere.

The closing chapter of Romans is about the church, specifically about *the people who make it work.* Verse 19 is the heart of that chapter:

> 19 For your obedience is come abroad unto all men. I am glad therefore on your behalf: but yet I would have you wise unto that which is good, and simple concerning evil.

Paul ended all his letters with words of greeting and personal exhortations and blessings. Romans is a highly theological work, but in the end—literally and figuratively—it was about people, because it was addressed to a real church. The last chapter of Romans is meant to encourage the Roman Christians to "keep on keeping on," so they would experience the victory of God.

Built Up by Encouragement
The first of several things Paul does in this chapter is to

acknowledge the faith, character and contribution of numerous persons in the Roman church. He does this because he knows that the people who make it work are *built up by encouragement.*

No less than twenty-six people are singled out by name for praise, in addition to several unnamed brethren or mothers, and hosts of others included in their "households." Paul wasn't hesitant to call their names for fear he would leave some out. He might not be able to name everyone who deserved mention, but if he mentioned no one, he would have done wrong.

The first name on the list is **Phebe** (we usually spell it *Phoebe*), described as **a servant of the church which is at Cenchrea** (v.1). Many other translations are bold to render the underlying Greek the same way it is many other places: "deacon"—or in this case, to preserve the gender of the word, deaconess.

The context of this verse indicates fairly clearly that Phebe was regarded to be one of the deacons of the Cenchrean church. If not, there was no reason to call her by the Greek word for deacon. If she were merely a servant in the way every believer is expected to be a servant, why mention it, unless Paul were going to detail how she had served exceptionally. Furthermore, she transported the letter of Paul to the Roman church, and apparently she had some matter of business there relating to ministry needs back home, a fact that Paul mentions in v.2.

Finally, Paul's description of her "service" is given in precisely the words we might expect to find of biblical deacons: **"She hath been a succourer of many, and of myself also"** (v.2). She had helped many in their time of distress. This practical service, not spiritual authority, is the biblical role of the deacon.

Just as Paul commends Phebe for her service, he has the warmest of greetings for **Aquila and Priscilla** (v.3), who **laid down their own necks** for him (v.4)—put themselves in jeopardy to defend him when he was pursued and persecuted.

Paul greets **the church that is in their house** (v.5), a phrase that is overwhelmingly believed to mean that a church *met* in their house. In view of the presumption reflected in this letter that the church in Rome was unified, this "house church" apparently was something like a satellite congregation, belonging to the larger church, but meeting on their own. Probably there were several such satellites throughout the city.

There are many other people mentioned in this chapter: some who worked for Paul's benefit or who were fellow prisoners at one time; some who were kin to Paul; and some who were just dear friends and supporters. The two women or girls, Tryphena and Tryphosa, may have been twins.

By listing all these, Paul encouraged them. On a purely human level, the sweetest sound to a person's ears is the sound of his own name. Also, everyone responds positively to praise. And even if we intend to redirect all praise to God, it is in our nature, and rightfully so, to be further motived by expressed appreciation. Most of us could do better in the praise and compliments department.

It used to be that movies began with the list of stars, cast, and the major people responsible for the movie—the director, producer, costumer, set designers, and a few others. Things may have begun to change when labor unions in Hollywood began to demand that the names of the grips and dolly movers and lighting assistants and assistants to assistants to casting crew helpers be put in the credits as well. Eventually the list had to appear at the end, because it was getting too long for people to wait through at the first of the film. Some of the credits seem a bit ridiculous—who would ever notice or remember some of the contributions made or jobs done, we might think.

But Joe Nobody, who did one of those forgettable jobs, will always wait through the credits and feel encouraged when his name rolls up. And it may make the difference in his continuing to contribute to the art.

Churches are no different. Christians are encouraged when they are praised for their work and their accomplishments. Encouraged Christians work harder, give more, and keep on keeping on.

Bettered by Discipline

As well as praise due, there was a need for some words of warning. Paul had apparently read the current books on good management techniques and knew that you should sandwich criticism between slices of praise! After he encouraged by praise, he issued some cautions, because he knew the people who make the church work are *bettered by discipline.*

In a very short word in v.17 Paul turns serious and tells the faithful in Rome to **mark them which cause divisions and offences.** "Mark" means identify them. The divisions and offenses they cause are about things Paul says are **contrary to the doctrine which ye have learned** (v.17). There were some people associated with the church in Rome who were trying to rewrite the doctrines of the word of God, introducing foreign ideas, liberalizing, compromising, or distorting. Such activity could not help but cause controversy.

This kind of destructive activity was not peculiar to Rome. It is one of Satan's favorite methods throughout the ages to destroy the evangelistic effectiveness of churches. He finds people who are resistant to the powerful truths of the gospel, or easily sidetracked by peripheral issues, and he induces them to mislead others.

These are the persons who are to be "marked" in our churches today. Make a mental note that such persons are divisive or theologically off-track. Then, following Paul's instructions, **avoid them** (v.17).

What does that mean? It sounds rather harsh when stated so bluntly; but what this means is that these people are to be kept from infecting the fellowship with their divisive words and actions.

The most serious cases of marking and avoiding would involve what we call "church discipline." Churches have performed this responsibility in different ways throughout history, sometimes more harshly than others. The Amish even today do what they call "shunning," in which a person who causes trouble is ignored, not spoken to, discounted in activities, for a certain period of time.

Perhaps their method is overly austere, and perhaps not.

But most of our churches don't even have a defined process in place to accomplish any sort of discipline. Neither would many churches accept it. The mood of many a church is characterized by a spirit of independence that is not highly receptive to the concept of spiritual authority in the congregation.

That doesn't change the fact that we really do need discipline occasionally, because as Paul says, there are some in the church who **serve not our Lord Jesus Christ** (v.18). Instead, they serve **their own belly** (v.18), which is a reference to the appetites that come from their worldly and sinful selves. These "belly" motives appear to revolve around the desire to receive attention or to be in charge. That Paul had to identify the real motives of these people who **caused division** was evidence that then, as now, some people can fool others into believing they are doing the Lord's bidding, when in fact they are wrecking crews destroying the Lord's true work.

Blessedly, the Roman church was not chock full of these divisive people at that particular time, for Paul typified them in the top piece of bread in the managerial sandwich of criticism: **Your obedience is come abroad unto all men** (v.19). The warning about people who caused division was more a caution than an implication of a life threatening condition. Still, he added, **yet I would have you wise unto that which is good, and simple concerning evil.** The contrast is between, on the one hand, knowing a lot about wisdom and being expert in exercising it, and on the other hand, knowing little of divisive and unbiblical ideas, and being decidedly inexperienced at causing trouble and turmoil.

Why don't we read this chapter more often?

Enabled by Grace

Encouragement is a positive motivation. Discipline may be seen as a more negative motivation but still with a constructive goal. Back in the seventh chapter, however, Paul had said, "To will is present with me; but how to perform that which is good I find not" (7:18). Motivation is necessary but by itself insufficient. Someone totally paralyzed cannot run, though he may want to badly.

The pivotal issue for Christians is how to do what we should do, both individually and together as the church. And Paul gives the answer, as the final word of the Roman letter: The people who make the church work are *enabled by grace.*

When Paul predicts that **the God of peace shall bruise Satan under your feet shortly** (v.20), he implies this will happen as they put into effect the discipline he has talked about, while remaining radically faithful to Christ in every other way. And the power to do all this is **the grace of our Lord Jesus Christ** (v.20), which he wishes and prays for them to experience.

This verse effectively closes the letter, but even as Paul adds "P.S.'s" to it, greetings from **Tertius,** who actually penned the letter for Paul, and hellos from others, he injects again this emphasis on grace: **The grace of our Lord Jesus Christ be with you all** (v.24). This is not merely "have a nice day" in Greek. It's a substantial desire for the grace of God to be received and experienced by the Romans. And the grace of God is itself very substantial for Paul and for all Christians. *Grace is the good gift of power from God sufficient to accomplish the will and desire of God in our lives.* A close, one-word equivalent would be "ability"—divine ability at work in us.

Our lives from here to eternity are unwritten, from our perspective. God knows what we will and will not accomplish. From our standpoint, however, we are obligated to seek the grace of God to: tackle the mission of the church; undertake the disciplines of the faith; develop the holiness God expects; acquire knowledge and understanding of his word; and do anything else he has laid out for us as responsibilities of the people of God.

But God **is of power to stablish you** (v.25), Paul says. His power comes through the gospel in particular, and through the **preaching of Jesus Christ** (v.25) in its fulness—in other words, God's power comes through God's word. We shouldn't be surprised that much of this enablement of grace comes through our study and knowledge of the **scriptures of the prophets** and the **commandment of the everlasting God** (v.26) found in the Bible. He has made the Bible one of the essential keys to what Paul calls **the obedience of faith** (v.26). That obedience is very simply the goal and the end of all humanity in God's plan.

Summing Up Romans

Paul's letter to the Romans describes in almost painstaking detail the gospel of Jesus Christ and how it works to bring us from sin to repentance, repentance to faith, faith to obedience, and obedience to maturity. In its final few phrases, the letter attempts to inspire the Roman believers to be caught up in the eternal drama of Christ's kingdom and coming glory. For after all the distractions and superficial pursuits of this temporary world have disappeared like morning fog into the brilliance of the everlasting day, only what we have become in Christ will be lasting.

But in the same way that the divine potter of Romans 9 **endured with much longsuffering the vessels of wrath** so as to **make his power known,** and also called out **vessels of mercy** toward whom he would **make known the riches of his glory,** so in the end God will be glorified no matter which path of life any individual chooses.

Some people will be found to have obeyed the gospel, to have followed Christ, and to have grown spiritually and done the will of God in varying degrees. Others will be found to have spurned the salvation of Christ and to have pursued their own plans, some more notoriously than others. But the dividing line will be sharp, not fuzzy. Judgment will find each of us on one side of that line, or the other.

Whether or not an individual obeys the gospel and follows through in faith all his life, ultimately the doxology that ends the letter will come true: **To God only wise, be glory through Jesus Christ for ever, Amen.** It is no small matter whose side we will be found to be on.

9780983464273